I'm Just Starting

A Reluctant Criminal's High Road to County Jail

Andrea M Gilson

I'm Just Starting 2

www.andreamgilson.com

I'm Just Starting 3

For Mustang

I'm Just Starting 4

www.andreamgilson.com

Acknowledgments

God does what he does in my life to serve my greater good to His purpose. Most often I do not know what He is doing, I trust that He does. Thanks be to God for these experiences. The people I encountered in jail that made the adventure possible deserve mention and I pray each has moved on to better circumstances. Thanks to the Nanowrimo (National Novel Writing Month) organization and staff for the forced deadline and the pep-talks.

I'm Just Starting 6

Prologue

I hope that my readers will be varied. It is my goal to give people hope if they are in similar situations and to have a point of reference of expectation. The body of the book deals with the crime and punishment turn that my life took for a few years of my mid-life. I have included appendixes to give further insight and help to the reader. Throughout the body stories are told and profiles of the main players in these stories are outlined in Appendix A. This is done so that the reader can either relate to them or better understand the phenomenon of crime. Appendix B gives personalities of the main officers that guarded and served us in the place I was held. This was included to offer respect for them and prove that officers are humans too. Some that read this book may be bitter toward the police and it is my goal to change that. Appendix C is my transcription of the exact notes I recorded during my jail stay. To retain the notes exactly without adding the aliases I have created for my characters throughout the book, the actual names have been written and then blacked out. It can be assumed that elsewhere in the book that the names have been changed. I believe these notes will be of interest because they are immediate in the moment and can teach others the benefits of note-taking. Whether my book is successful or not, my pages of hand-written notes will remain in my scrapbooks for years. Appendix D is the basic Gospel of Jesus Christ. I do not mean to exclude anyone that is of opposing faiths but it is my responsibility to tell others of Him who helped me through this adventure and through life. I certainly want others to gain the freedom that comes with trusting in Him. Appendix E is the twelve steps of Alcoholics Anonymous. Regardless of an individual's faith, these steps are vital tools for living and for shrugging off the hells of addiction. Scripture verses are sprinkled within the text. This serves to show how God's word can help people to cope and to edify them throughout life's circumstances and to introduce those that are not familiar with the Bible to see for themselves that the content is varied and it is not at all boring.

Introduction

Sometimes good people use bad judgment. When they use bad judgment consistently, then they become bad people. The police, the court, and God worked together to stop this criminal from getting worse. Jail was one of those things that happened to other people, bad people. Alcohol played the main character in this saga. I let it for years. No more. I named this book what I did because bad behavior was not my environment throughout life and therefore, my criminal record was earned reluctantly. Indeed, after spending time in jail, I found that mine was the high road. Kind of like a high bottom. Going rather unknowingly and unwillingly down the bad road to worse fates, I emerged back on track to sobriety and respectability. Two DUI convictions landed me in jail. It was really the second that landed me in jail. But if I had not been guilty of the first misdemeanor, there would have been no accumulative offender troubles.

Of all the crimes committed among my pod-mates, DUI was the least frequent offense. It made me feel a little better. I am certainly not trying to say that DUI crimes are a light matter, only that those crimes were not conscious decisions and the types of crime I encountered in jail required forethought and planning. Included in these were bad check writing and counterfeiting. My decision to stop drinking alcohol will allow me to make conscious decisions in the future, hopefully ones that will please my God and earthy father especially.

Regret and guilt are useless emotions. Nonetheless, they play a role in most people's life at some point. This story attempts to place the years of my early forties and when I earned the criminal record I now hold in perspective. It is ineligible to be sealed or removed. The seventy-five year time frame means that the crimes I committed will follow me wherever I go, forever. This story should never have happened. Life has a way of taking each of us down these roads though. I separate the book into sections hoping that the reader will read them in order, however; the details of the jail stay may have some turning to that section. It seems sensationalistic if you've never been. It was not unlike an adventure experience. I now can say, been there-done that. If it happened, I may as well put a positive spin on it, there's no taking any of it back.

The memories of the experiences as a whole are meant to be therapeutic for me and can answer concerns to those that like me had no idea what to expect when my time came. I expect that within the binding of this book will be my entire criminal experience from start to finish. It was alright but like growing up in Buffalo, I am done with it.

This road was in Florida where the culture of those living close to the sea draws folks toward adopting an attitude of just have fun, its vacation, even if it isn't. A humorous phrase kind of says it all, "Where the debris meets the sea." This has become my go-to phrase for wanting to leave Florida. There is also the anecdote that Florida is the bilge of the nation. By looking at a map of the country, it is kind of fitting. I surely am insulting thousands of Florida residents with these past lines; I hope they can understand that this has only been my personal experience. It does explain why the police here are so zealous though, they must agree with me.

Years ago when I lived in Texas, I visited Daytona Beach while touring the Florida coast by car. I was stopped for speeding and the officer was quite rude. I tried to joke with him that since I had just been at the track that I had the need for speed. Instead of smiling at my clever joke, he warned me that if I failed to pay the ticket that the state of Florida would find me in Texas and take my license. Welcome to Florida, how rude. This was my first encounter with the police anywhere and I had lived in other states so please let me vent off on the Florida system. I was very insulted. I was no criminal how dare he imply that I would be delinquent in my responsibility to pay. He assumed I was a criminal; they are used to the debris landing in Florida I reckon. I plan to leave Florida behind.

I chose to write this story or sequence of events really so that my readers can see that there is always the bright side of any circumstance. The events and characterization in this story are real. The names of the people I will introduce are made up by me for reasons which will become obvious since I plan to be frank. I want this story to be told, I want to get the fact that this happened to me off of my conscious, and I plan to make it entertaining.

With all of that introductory mumbo- jumbo taken care off, here is the short of it. I lived over forty years as a moderate, responsible, involved member of society. I was raised properly by a military father, to whom I owe the world. My upbringing helped me to see that I did not belong in jail as most of my pod-mates seemed to accept the situation as part of the norm. I learned about Christ young and loved him my whole life. I certainly made him frown a lot when I was putting more importance on having as much fun as possible in as little time as possible for the years I lived in Florida. In Florida that is what people do, they have fun. It is where people go to escape, right? Since I have been here it is interesting that most everyone I talk to that is from elsewhere wants to leave. The people that were born and raised here seem to like it; they do not have anything to compare it to. It is depressing even though the sun is always out.

The police in the Sunshine State are not very forgiving, which I understand more than ever now after intimacy with the personality types they must deal with daily. My original ranting is tempered by my firsthand experience with other people that live here and keep the police busy and surely at their wit's end. They take their job seriously and I am grateful that they arrested me when I drove around my city rather unconsciously; I reckon, if the BAC (Blood Alcohol Content) is any real indicator. After my public defender advised me to accept the state's sentence of thirty days in jail, I did just that. The alternative would have been wearing a bracelet around my ankle and not leaving the house. I thought that would be dreadful and strangely considered a month in the county jail as a type of adventure. It was exactly that but not at all what I had expected. I had asked anyone I could to give me the low-down but I do not know any criminals so no one knew anything. That statement may be a denial since I did glean tips from somewhere. I must have known someone who knew. I was loved at work so the absence there was worked out fine, as a matter of fact; my generous boss wrote a letter to my judge asking for clemency since I was vital to him. The judge did not think so and that was that. The judges are limited in a lot of cases. Punishment for a DUI crime is often not in the judge's hands to decide. I served the state-mandatory required time for my act. Still, I could not believe that I was officially a criminal. How crass.

Daddy was quite supportive and took my news with a good attitude. Of course, I tried to keep it from him like I have done with other shameful events in my past. After it happened and we would speak on the phone and he asked me if anything was new, I would just give him the sedate details of my days skimming over the big news. His voice each time he asked caused me to think that he might be onto me, so I told him finally. As I suspected, he already knew. The news got through to him through my sister. Blimy, I thought my secrets were safe with her. Thankfully many still are. Not this time. Even with his middle daughter now a jail-time serving criminal, Daddy is proud of me for the things I have done positively in my life. He reminds me each time I talk to him and I consider things I do more heavily now knowing I have to make this story up to him.

The jail stay was only a fraction of the many penalties I was faced with but I systematically submitted to them until I was free from my probation a year later. Even more harrowing was the fact that I lost my driver's license for five years. Already cozily accustomed to going without a car for so long, I wonder what the big deal is. I have made friends with the bus system and lost tons of weight riding my bike. The environment is happy with me too. But again, this story teller will try to disregard the Florida legal system at large except where the hands-on experience calls the officers and procedures of the county jail into memory.

In a way I was graced, God did not abandon me. Even though he was disappointed like my daddy, he supported me through the challenges. I was in the middle of the college semester. At my initial court date, an agreement was made between the court and my public defender that I would remain free until after I finished this coursework and then turn myself in officially at that time.   I did have to pass on a summer class which put me behind enough to miss the graduation ceremony one year later but I got my degree, just a few months late is all. I blame that just as much on my advisors false curriculum promises as the missed summer class. Like I already mentioned, everything happens for a reason that God knows about. I do not necessarily have to know what He is doing. My spring grades did suffer a bit because of the stress but not badly enough to damage my GPA. Anyway, May 15th arrived in no time.

I treated it like a vacation. I arranged for a neighbor to get my mail and water my plants. My date of reckoning arrived and I woke up with a tinge of fear but dressed to impress the judge and look like the non-criminal that I was/am. I wore my Roswell shoes in case they got lost in the shuffle. The Roswell shoes should have been discarded long ago but they are still by my door being used regularly. I bought them in Roswell, New Mexico after my hiking shoes proved painful. Now they held souvenir value, plus they were comfortable. The seams are ripping, they are badly scuffed and they have black fire damage streaks on them. I am moving to Oregon in a few months and am undecided if I should finally part with them. I was over-joyed when I slid them back onto my feet after the days of assigned footwear inside.

Still, even with a record and a history of jail time, I do not believe I am a criminal. I was basically unconscious when I drove around oblivious. So I guess I am a unconscious criminal. The whole event scared me quite badly into realizing I had been endangering innocents unknowingly. This story and the stigma I personally feel because of it ensure that I will do no more crimes, consciously or not. To guarantee it, I have put the pleasures of imbibing aside. I know there really can be no guarantee in life about anything but I will do my part to lower the chances of crime sneaking up on me unawares. I had to squash the phrase I spoke to my pod-mates in my first minutes with them that "I'm just starting." Good grief, I thought, why in the world would I say that. I don't want that to end up being some obscure prophesy. So I will certainly also be "Just ending"- my criminal career- upon my release.

Part One- The start

I'm Just Starting 16

Chapter One

A normal person may have grasped that it was not necessarily normal to grab a six-pack of beer before the party started. Thinking about it now, it probably would sound normal to the group of people I had made my circle at this point. I drank a can of beer on the drive home to get changed, another while showering, and finished one off in the parking lot before going in. Just a few hours earlier while finishing up my duties at work, my friend asked if I planned on getting drunk that night. My answer was "Hell yeah." Why did this sound right to me? Simple, for a period of some years I loved alcohol more than common sense. The party was great. I felt a little worried when I first went in and greeted my big boss. I had enough already but enjoyed more beer during the party and after. At least I gorged on the buffet which was a blessing. A part of my crime the second time was not eating a morsel before or while imbibing, very stupid.

Noticing that my favorite place to have a beer(s) with friends had cleared out, I asked Bill, my friend and co-worker what time it was getting to be. "One-thirty," we both said in unison once he pulled up his sleeve to expose his wrist. Since we both had to be at work in six hours, we left quickly. A Christmas party earlier in the evening was the usual obligatory socializing and many of my friends had wanted to stay out.

We headed off. He made it to work, I did not. I now know that the most common reasons the police stop people late at night is because they either do not have their lights on or they are speeding. I was guilty of trying to get home to bed as fast as possible. I suppose the police have a habit of waiting outside of popular drinking holes when it is close to last call to get people like me off the street. This is what happened to me. I had just pulled out, made my right turn and drove about a quarter mile before the police scared me to death with their bubble lights. They gave me just enough time to start speeding home and boom.

I drank lite beer that night and I do not know how many. I told the officers it was about fifteen and they were incredulous. I believe it was right on. They asked me if there was anything in my car that they should know about. I told them there was a cooler in the back with some beer in it. Who but a person with an alcohol problem has beer at the ready in a cooler in the car? I thought I was smart in never having open containers in my car. I had always been a stickler for that. It was really just God looking out for me knowing I was in enough trouble already. My friends thought this truthful disclosure was hilarious.

I failed the roadside test and did not think anyone could do the feats they required. At the time I thought I had done okay following the pen with my eyes and touching my nose with my finger from first one side and then the other. It was the standing on one foot (impossible) and walking the line with one foot placed flush in front of the other that betrayed my condition. Some people thought I should have used my former stroke as an excuse for failing these tests. While it is true, I have balance issues because of it- that did not help me later with the BAC. I did not think of my medical history at that time anyway, I had more important things on my mind like, "where are they taking my car?"

I did not have to blow into a breathalyzer yet. They wanted to wait until the booze hit my system really well before testing me. I do not know why they waited, that was my guess. Before long I was sitting in a squad car watching a tow truck pull my car away. This was a trauma. I was polite but nearly panicked wondering what would happen to my car. These officers were helpful, they had written the name of the company on a card and placed it in my purse so I could figure it out the next day. I was above the legal limit to be driving but was coherent enough to remember and quite cooperative if not confused. As we drove away and headed farther from familiar streets, I told the police that if it was all the same to them, they could just drop me at a cheap motel so that I could walk to work in the morning. I did not get it. It did not dawn on me for a long time that they were taking me to spend the night in jail. Next thing I knew, we headed onto the freeway. I remember asking many times, "Where are we going?" We seemed to drive forever. I blankly stared out the rear window watching the pavement race away from me.

I think it was clear to these cops that I was a novice criminal. Genuine confusion gripped me. I had no idea what was going on. I am sure the night's drinking did not help. The officers that [helped me] were polite. They took me into a small room where a young complaining man was spewing expletives. I had to sit next to him. His ranting made me insane and I told him to just get a grip already. I was pretty brave. Twice I looked at him and scolded him for his behavior. Was I subconsciously trying to make brownie points? A female officer had to go with me to the toilet. Worse, she had to unbuckle my belt since I was cuffed. The cuffs hurt my wrists. I wish I would have remembered that better.

No road side breathalyzer test was given but now I moved to a desk with a big officer asking me questions. He taught me how to blow into the device. It reminded me of the device patients blow into at the hospital to test their breathing force. I gave it my all, I think he thought I over-did it like I was trying to blow down the house. I probably did this as a flashback from the many times I had to prove to the nurses in the hospital how ready I was to go home. At this point, he told me that I would have my license taken away for at least six months. Until this time I was sad but reserved. With the new development, I burst into tears. Generally quite unemotional, this reminded me of the time at the flight academy when they informed me that my base assignment would be JFK airport in New York. I had gone through the process to get to a warmer climate. New York was the last choice on my preference list. I burst into tears. It did not happen very often.

This made my arrest photo very attractive with black mascara raccoon eyes. When I got back to my life, I couldn't believe (I really could) that my friends had been laughing at my mug shot the whole time. One of my closest friends even put it on his phone so that it came up when I called him. How compassionate they all were.

After I finished in this area, I moved to the county holding center. I do not think we drove anywhere new. It is amazing how multi-functional the complex is. This giant room of diverse folk held the people that broke the law and were arrested that night. Rows upon rows of seats attached to the floor occupied the main section in the middle of the room. Along the edges were offices for further processing like medical and ID badges. There were more but those were the only two I got subjected to this night. Overseeing officers stood against the wall only breaking their post to chit-chat with the others or lead a group of inmates into a further abyss. Circular phone stations were near the restrooms. Only the seasoned could figure out how to use the phones. Twice I went to them and attempted to make a call, no good. I was a holding center phone idiot.

It was cold and I was not allowed to lie down but had to remain sitting. It might have been worse. I was grateful that I am a conservative dresser. Long pants and long sleeves saved me from hypothermia. Part of the entertainment was getting my inmate identification badge, talking to medical personnel, and getting fed two peanut butter and honey sandwiches. They were great. I honestly had never had a peanut butter and honey sandwich before. It must be a southern thing.

I did not inform anyone about my plight until I was released. At one point, a judge told me from a TV screen that I could go home on my own recognizance. He looked over his notes and asked me in statement form, "You have never been arrested before." I simply said, "No." I was suddenly very ashamed of myself for getting into trouble for the first time at age forty-one. Chivalry was alive in the court. Even though several men had been seated in the room prior to our entering, the women got first priority with the judge. It was a challenge to all involved when an inmate did not understand or speak English. Interpreters were summoned and we moved forward.

We filed from the smaller room and I was sent back into the big room where everyone waited to hear what would imminently become their fate. I commiserated with those near me. I found that most of them knew exactly what to expect and made this journey frequently. They reassured me after I recounted my circumstances to them.

I was released uneventfully with my purse restored to me. I did not notice until much (days) later that my license had been removed from my wallet stealthily. I was offended at this. Why didn't they just ask me to turn it over or at least tell me that they had gone through my stuff? Oh yeah, I was a criminal now with no rights. I had not forgotten what the man at the desk had said about losing my privilege, but did not expect them to lift my property. That might have been a wrongful assumption now that I recall. Maybe it was only on loan to me as long as I was not a law-breaker. Aha, it all makes sense now. Even so, I felt the police were sneaky. I learned that even though I did not think of myself as a criminal, they certainly did.

I do not know how much time I spent getting processed but I know I was arrested about 1:30am and when I was picked up by one of my friends it was the next evening about 7:00pm. Bad at math, I suppose that is about eighteen hours altogether. Leaving the building behind me when I exited, I was disoriented. I got scolded for not going the right way as if I knew where I was. I was no professional criminal; I was just starting. My buddy Jay graciously fetched me from the courthouse (not so affectionately called, The Court Hotel) and let me talk his ear off as he drove me home. Looking at the name of the company that had towed my car away several hours earlier, I recognized the name as a friend's family business. I quickly called this man- the same person that asked me the evening prior if I had planned on getting drunk at the party. He sympathized with me for a while but told me that his folks no longer owned that automobile shop. I was out of luck.

It was a hunt the next day to secure my car back to me even though I knew where it was. I went immediately to the impound yard and saw my car behind the lock in. The owner was nice but sent me to the police station for some documentation. When I went in there I felt really ignored. I stood at the glass window waiting for attention for what seemed like forever. Of course, this was my faulty perspective. I wanted my car back. According to my ticket, I had ten days to drive. I lived on the bus line at this time (and miraculously the second time) making my transportation problems greatly reduced. This was so clearly the work of God as to be impossible to deny. I change apartments often and both times I was arrested for DUI and without personal transportation, the bus stop was mere steps from my door. No coincidence. God loves me and so do my friends.

 I learned that I had many friends when I no longer could drive. They were available to take me where I needed to go and the obligations that pile up from the conviction never seemed to end. A funny thing about the whole ordeal was that the authorities knew that if you had a DUI you probably were not driving yet they make it so that every different part of the loose ends to be tied up to satisfy the punishment had to be taken care of at all opposite sides and directions within the county.   I am sure that the county and the public bus system are in cahoots with one another.

Here is what my punishment ended up as. I accepted later as the reader will find that these steps were nothing but an inconvenience in the larger picture: loss of driver privilege for six months, probation for one year, $600 fine, fifty hours of community service, a DUI safety council course, ten weeks of counseling, and car impound for one week. The cost was substantial. Probation alone cost $50 for every visit. The impound was the most harrowing punishment I endured. Others got out of this hellish procedure by claiming that another person relied on their car for transportation. I alone used my car and since I do not lie, I had to go through with it. My honesty had caused me to shoot myself in the foot at other times in my life as well. I know that if I had lied, I would get punished two-fold for my trouble by God.

The sheriff's office had to affix a glaring orange sticker to the rear window of my car and it had to be parked (by someone else, since I could not drive) and not moved for an entire week. The car had to be brought to the sheriff's office for the operation so I had to enlist someone to drive my car there. I learned while being processed (I hate that phrase) that my registration was missing. This was a true snag. When I bought my car, the dealer said they would handle the registration and they did-almost. I never received a piece of paper to keep in my wallet like I did in other states. I always wondered about that. In reality I should have had one as the sheriff now delayed my progress because of it. Nor was there a sticker in my window, just on the rear plate. My poor unsuspecting friend now wasted more of his day driving me all over the place to replace my missing registration paper. Nothing went smoothly it seemed. I could tell he was flustered but he was a good sport.

It just so happened that I could not even back the car up against the bushes which was my first agenda. I was scolded recently from others at the condo because they had a stupid rule (one among many) that said everyone had to part uniformly nose in. Surveillance of the impound was threatened, so I did what the police wanted and all of my neighbors in the condo building that I lived in were privy to my DUI arrest. I can picture a gossipy group of them standing by my car while I was at work reading the small print. On the seventh day, I went out in the rain, in the dark with a blade to remove it. To me at that point, it never happened. The sticker was gone? What sticker? I am sure everyone in that building had a cocktail party to celebrate when I moved out.

I enjoyed my community service more than I should have. I made and served food at an American Legion post. I never had so much free food. I took stacks of containers home every Friday and Saturday.

It was hardly punishment; we had a blast working in that kitchen. Sadly, just a few months later one of the men I volunteered (?) with died. I do not know the circumstances but he was very young. I suspect that he did not give up his addictive lifestyle and fell further into the abyss. I think this because a few others that I have known through the AA program that were healthy except for their relapses also died too young. I have good memories of him from the kitchen.

I qualified for a hardship license since I worked full-time and I also attended college full-time. So I really was without my license for only a month. The hardship replacement cost over $200 and it had to be paid in cash. Ever without cash, I had to find an ATM machine nearby while the overseer waited. The compact long-haired woman had eternal patience and I liked her because she granted my request. If she had wanted to she could have made me return on a different day with the cash, she was the understanding type. Who carried cash nowadays? My new license arrived in the mail with a new indicator on it. It said 'business purposes' only and the date that its full privilege would kick in. I was surprised to learn that when the months expired that I could get a replacement without the indicator for no cost. This is the first time anything official would be offered at no cost. I never got it changed anyway.

Probation was no problem. Bill who had been with me the night of my arrest helped me get to the appointments. It was funny watching him try to plug the address into his car's GPS. By the time he figured it out, we were there. My boss allowed a flexible schedule so I did not have to haggle with my probation officer about appointment dates made in advance.

At the first session, myself and others were shown a video and listened to a lecture about the probation process. After that I simply had to show up and pay my money. I made an appointment for the next month and that was it. My probation was based on my finishing all of the stipulations of my punishments and was able to get reduced in time if I was vigilant. I was and my probation self-terminated after six months. It was probably more painful for my friend that acted as my chauffeur.   I had not yet become fully intimate with the county public bus.

There was the DUI offender counseling session. It was a weekend class lasting twelve hours. It was close to home. A police officer taught the class. We watched many movies and had to take a breathalyzer each day right after lunch. It was amazing that people actually got caught drinking when they were there to straighten out a substance abuse conviction. These are the ones with real trouble. There was a woman in my class that seemed so frazzled and incoherent that I could not believe it when she passed the breath test. She might have had a mental condition because she was like a lunatic. She seemed wasted on drugs to me.

After the certificate was granted that I finished the course, I had to undertake an evaluation to decide whether or not further counseling was needed. The beige certificate looks like a diploma worthy of framing. Some day as a joke maybe I will take this one and my second one and add them to my office wall with my legitimate degrees and accomplishment diplomas. If the observer doesn't look to close, maybe I will just appear more scholarly for the quantity of framed documents. To my surprise, the interviewer sentenced me to ten weeks of additional counseling. I did not see that coming. It would cost thirty-five dollars each time. It is hard not to imagine the whole situation as a conspiracy for the county and affiliates to make money. In reality, the lady that sent me to further classes saw into my soul, because given the continuing saga, she saw the truth.

Thinking about all the stress I put myself through at the time, it was really nothing. In time, I carelessly drank and drove again.

Chapter Two

Since I am getting all of my brushes with the law out of the way in one full sweep, I should recount the drunken walking episode. I was not quite as cooperative this time. After my DUI, I wanted nothing to do with drinking- for a few months. Then the rules I laid out became laxer and laxer for myself. I would stick to only three beers if I went out with my friends. Years earlier I had decided to drink only beer when in public; this was because I used to love red wine. I would be falling off of stools and my friends had to grudgingly baby-sit me. The embarrassment led me to set the beer only rule for myself. I thought that would keep me out of trouble. I kept that rule for a long time but in the end it failed. I know now that I had developed a real problem with alcohol and it was going to tell me what to do.

Written mainly by the wise man Solomon, the scriptural book of Proverbs addresses the power of alcohol's influence. "Who hath woe? Who hath sorrow? Who hath contentions? Who hath babbling? Who hath wounds without cause? Who hath redness of eyes? [29] They that tarry long at the wine; they that go to seek mixed wine.[30] Look not thou upon the wine when it is red, when it giveth its color in the cup, when it moveth itself aright. [31] At the last it biteth like a serpent, and stingeth like an adder.[32] Thine eyes shall behold strange women, and thine heart shall utter perverse things. [33] Yea, thou shalt be as he that lieth down in the midst of the sea or as he that lieth upon the top of a mast. [34] They have stricken me, shalt thou say, and I was not sick, they have beaten me, and I felt it not; when shall I awake? I will seek it yet again[35] (Proverbs 23:29-35 KJV). The oblivion of drunkenness is a strong lure that often causes one to return time and again despite the consequences.

On a rainy night at a club listening to a band and eating wings I made off for home on foot. I did not tell my friends I was leaving; I was just suddenly tired and bored. Earlier in the night, I had accepted an invitation to set off for a few different places. I was very smart to leave my car at home and went in someone else's car. I was trying real hard not to drink and drive. My home was not far from where I was when I got tired, so I abandoned my friends and headed for the street. I had not gone six blocks when my town's finest pulled up and an officer approached me. He said I was weaving all over and could injure myself by falling into traffic. Really, I thought, fall into traffic? I was on the sidewalk; I would have had to jump into traffic. I had heard everything now.

I had been truly proud of my responsibility in leaving my car at home. What made me mad was that I lived only a few more blocks from where this occurred. Instead of these men driving me home and leaving me with a scare, they drove me ten miles away to a holding shelter to dry up. I had to hit up the ATM for a cash advance to pay for the $50 cab ride home. All I did at this place was sit at a desk and complain to my new care-takers. The man and woman were sympathetic and called me a cab very soon after I was dropped off. I could not believe I would get punished for being so smart. I since learned that being smart is drinking club soda mixed with cranberry juice and a lime. So while I did not get arrested that night, I might as well have. I was mad.

The police have no sympathy. They had to teach me a lesson instead of taking me the few blocks home. I think I have it figured out now. They are not stupid like us criminals. They decided that if they took me home that I would just get in my car and drive somewhere. Maybe they were right. I had not been unruly but vocally persistent in my innocence. Wasn't I supposed to walk home after I had a few too many. Yeah, I was mad.

Part Two- DUI #2

I'm Just Starting 30

Chapter Three

I have been arrested once before for a DUI. Unfortunately for me on so many levels, it was less than two years prior to the new one. Much has been written by this author about that first crime. It was my first crime ever. The judge even seemed impressed with this on the little portable TV screen used in the co-ed room on my first day in holding after my first arrest. He was lenient and I was released on my own recognizance. I was very cooperative since I was raised to respect authority. I even titled the play I wrote about the experience *Cooperative Female*. The point I am making here is that my punishment for that first charge was too lenient. Now I can hear the cries of people who disagree with me about the toughness of DUI law in Florida. I am saying that if I had the consequences the first time that I suffered the second time, there would have been no second time.

I do not want to act like a hero and say that I wanted more punishments but in hindsight, the hoops I had to jump through then were a mere inconvenience. The caution I harbored for months afterward, slowly faded as the fun times returned. I followed many rules that I set down for myself, but alcohol has a way of over-ruling the rules. Making sound choices is not possible when you are in an unsound mind. I was beyond guilty when I was arrested the second time.

It was a Sunday. I was in class which was a film festival series that I had to analyze and write about. Nine straight days of taking notes on movies left me burnt out. I will never forget the movie of the day. It was animated about bears and the environment. When I turned on my phone and got a message from my former boyfriend about meeting for a drink, I was ready. We met and I was happy to see that he was wearing the shirt and necklace that I had bought him for his most recent birthday. This looked like a sign to me. We sat at an outside venue talking and smoking. Our relationship was not healthy. All we ever did was go to sporting events (very good) or bars (not so good). One indicator was that when we started dating neither of us smoked cigarettes, but by the time we broke up we both did. We must have been making each other nuts.

I had been enjoying those fruity liquor drinks that seem so innocuous. I generally stuck to lite beer (one of my rules), but the get together with Jimmie distracted me. This is my excuse, it is the only one I have. A really dumb thing to do is to drink something when you have no idea what is in it. I learned later that my delicious fruity treats had six (yes six) shots of various liquors in each. Shouldn't that be illegal? We had frequented this place every month or so but every other time I had gone there with him as his girlfriend, this time I drove myself and met him there as a friend. I was unaware of the consequences since I always just sat in the passenger seat afterward serenely comfortable, taking it easy without the responsibility of driving. That evening, I had only had two drinks and my BAC put me nearer to death than I can imagine. Class had ended at five o'clock and I was arrested about eight. I poisoned myself well.

The last memory I have before the police scene was of walking to the parking garage with Jimmie. I said, "It's funny that we got parking spots right next to each other." I wonder if I had been bouncing off of the sides of that winding parking garage exit ramp when I left. My car showed no damage but the route is tough even if sober. I drove quite far before the police stopped me. The hand of God was with me.

My clearest memory from the driving event was the tall bald officer repeating, "That taxi driver said that you hit him." I kept thinking, well if you were following me, don't you know? I said that I did [not] and where were my cigarettes anyway. I used to smoke only when I drank and thankfully since I no longer drink, I also no longer smoke. Good things come from bad things. The officer was correct. There were none left. I know because I looked for them in my car later. I do not know if I wanted to smoke or wanted to see if he had been lying. I figured he may be just telling me there were none in the car because he had other problems with me than waving a cigarette while he gave me the roadside test. I dozed after I was placed in the squad car because I do not remember much until finding myself seated in that horrible big holding room. Men and women sat in all states. Some half asleep, others mumbling to themselves, some staring at the floor, and all looking like they had better days. In this room it was freezing. Some of the girls had been scantily dressed at the time of their arrests and already wore jailhouse garb. It would have been dangerous for them to wait in a room full of men ogling them or worse in their short-shorts and halter tops. Fortunately, I was cold most of the time and my clothes were not a threat. I was still cold though. I tried to lay my head and arms across my body as I kept my feet on the floor.

An officer was always handy to yell, "Feet on the floor," if anyone tried to lie across the seats. It made it difficult to sleep but I suppose they wanted everyone awake until a call for medical, meals, release, or a move to an area with a mattress. The good thing about the position I assumed is that it is the natural position a person might take to keep from vomiting, perfect in my case. There were TVs in the room but the volume was turned down so it was like watching silent movies. Part of the entertainment was talking to the others about what the characters on the screen were saying. I think I stayed in this room for about six hours. I had my picture taken for my inmate badge, and had fun talking to the photographer about my former career as a flight attendant and the traveling I had done. I liked the photographer officer. He treated me like a person even though he saw scores of law breakers every night. I hope he knew I was not a real criminal. I can say that I was better dressed, I have all my teeth, I articulate well, and except the alcohol on my breath, I smelled pretty good. I had been out trying to impress a former boyfriend after all.

The phones are confusing and I doubt that anyone except the seasoned makes a call out at this point. Of course, cell phones are taken away. It is a bad thing that phone numbers get stored in the phone's memory and no longer in the human's brain. The only phone number I know without looking it up is my own. Technology is making us stupider. Phone books were available but they did no good. Everyone that an inmate would want to reach has a cell phone which is not listed in the books. Useless. In this initial holding area, the use of the bathroom is a universal affair. Whenever the officer feels like it, he/she makes a general call for the men or the women to line up for the toilet. They then stand half in and half out of the door as if to babysit us while we pee. A few people are allowed into the tri-toilet area at once. This is the first time for trying to see what you look like after your ordeal. The mirrors are that mystery compound that looks like stainless steel but has a faint element of reflection in it. I reckon that using real mirrors might tempt a would-be glass shard assailant. The toilets themselves are not at all unattractive. The trouble is they only have the bowl but no topping seat. It is one piece. I am sure these are stainless steel. If I weren't in jail, I may shop for one of this type for my own home. The sink nozzles were tiny but forceful. I think the county wasted a lot of water. In the past, some criminal might have figured out a way to make a weapon out of the screen so now the water just comes charging out.

     I noticed that these officers really had the life. Most were over-weight and basically babysat the people in the room. Some sat at high-chaired desks and others leaned against the walls bored. It seems like a rather depressing and brainless job. I stayed in this area for two meals. It must have been a while. At each meal, carts were brought in and juice and two sandwiches were handed out to each person. Bologna and cheese on white bread with a packet of mustard in cellophane was the main course. I loved the food. I also ate sandwiches that I saw still wrapped but abandoned on the chairs. I rarely met any food that I did not like.

     Out of boredom and surprise at seeing a clean attractive man among the dozens of people in the room, I brazenly started flirting with a stocky brown-haired man with tattoos peeking out from his short sleeves. This was beyond absurd and I knew it. Since everyone in the room was charged with some crime or another, picking up a man in a holding room wreaks of desperation. He politely answered a few of my inquiries and when he was onto me, he simply moved seats. Well, excuse me. He was a lot smarter than me. I enjoyed looking at him while I had the chance. He was removed with a group of men to a sleeping area a short while later. There seemed to be a sort of interview process before going into overnight rooms. I wonder if this was so that the officer could get the feel for the individual's demeanor before deciding where to place each and whom to place them with. I doubt they really give the process that much thought but I was daydreaming about why we were interviewed individually. I could not think of any other reason. As I sat with a group watching some James Brolin movie overhead, my name was called to go to the desk at the edge of the room. A skinny, high-voiced male officer in plain clothes talked to me about nothing in particular and told me to go line up by the far wall. I was miffed. Shouldn't I be sent home instead?

My BAC was too high for a release and I learned soon that I would have to actually bail myself out. I followed the group of girls and we changed clothes and got the basic toiletries. My sleeping room for the night was nice. I had a semi-private bunk. It really was not even a bunk but a slab on the floor where I placed a portable mattress. Although about six girls shared this room, dividers between each gave a fair measure of privacy. The shower area was big. One female officer guarded us. She was nice. She helped me when I asked her how I went about bailing myself out. She gave me the necessary number and taught me how to use the phone. That sounds silly, but it is no small comfort when in a strange environment.

The officer had less patience with a long-haired girl that was yelling at her mother on the phone. She yelled for her mother to calm down and she was yelling louder than anything. Patience is not the strongest trait of those in jail. I learned more with each new adventure experience. Again we were served yummy food. I may have lost track of time because I think I ate two meals in this holding cell also. It must have been my BAC; they really wanted me to get cleaned out before hitting the street. I was shocked that most of the girls threw their food into the trash. They must have known they would be out of there soon and would go order a pizza or something, but what a waste. I asked for a couple of their portions the second meal before watching it slide into the bin.

Eventually, we got called into a room where men were already seated. This would be another episode in front of the absent judge on the TV. Even though it had been quite a while since my arrest and I had eaten much, I suddenly felt sicker than ever. I wanted a glass of water so bad. To keep from vomiting I put my head between my knees. The alcohol must have just surfaced. The officers must be knowledgeable about the timing of this type of thing. Good thing they did not let me out yet. I needed sleep right now more than anything. I suffered through this session thinking I would embarrass myself and puck all over. I dizzily stood and the judge sternly asked me about my criminal history. Obviously not as impressed as the judge at my last arrest, I was now a repeat DUI offender. A miscreant. He said I could leave with $500 bail to wait for my court date. The fruity drinks were costing me a lot of money; a lot more than money too. Upon return to the semi-private cell, I called a bail bondsman right across the street from the county complex. They were so helpful and said they would make the arrangements with the jail and that I should be called for release by noon. I had to promise to go directly to their office to pay. I told them I had my credit card and would have to charge it. They were pleased and I laid down in the quiet and dozed.

I awoke to my escort ready to get me dressed back into my street clothes. They gave me back my belongings. My cell phone was the most precious at the time. Faintly irritated but reasonable I listened to a voice message from the man I had been out with just minutes before my arrest. He said, "Are you okay? I was a little worried about you after you left. Did you get home alright?" I suppose the sediment would have been more helpful before he placed me in my car and sent me on my way, but better late than never. He and I are still friends and I recognize my responsibility to look after myself.

Nevertheless, I often wish he had driven me home instead. I feel madder at him when he does not show any remorse at the dire situation I found myself in afterward than really blaming him for it. I guess I wanted a little commiseration from him. I got the best in the end. I do not drink alcohol anymore and as far as I am concerned, that is the best prize. God knew I had to be dealt with firmly. At this writing, two years have passed and I have not wanted to drink yet. I certainly can say one hundred percent that it is not worth it. I didn't even win the boyfriend back.

It was mid-morning when I walked out into the sunlight. I quickly found the bail bondsman (bondswoman) across the street. The white-haired woman that greeted me was thin and treated me very nicely. I did not feel like a criminal in her office even though I was there for collateral reasons. Thankfully, I could afford to pay the bail with my credit card. There was another $100 on top of the $500 to satisfy the bond. The woman gave me a tiny magnetic calendar to place on my fridge as a reminder to call her once a week as an assurance that I had not skipped town. I could have called her from Timbuktu. I was embarrassed that the calendar's face was the name of the Bail agent. I kept it on the fridge until court but then threw it away. It blared criminal. I thought of the check for $500 I received after my court date like found money. I was free for a while at least. I knew all of my friends would be at work so I called my roommate. He picked me up. I do not think he was surprised at my arrest. My roommates have always been the ones to see me at my worst.

I had no idea where my car was. I called the police and they said if it was not damaged they would have just left it parked. Well, that helped me a lot. I do not know where I had been driving. I studied my three tickets to narrow down the search perimeter. It seems the police followed me and infracted me all over the place. My roommate drove me around until we found my car. She (my cars are female) looked none the worse for wear and I drove her home. This made me nervous. Was I supposed to be driving? The police had taken my license. I justified myself since it said on the back of one of my tickets that I could drive for ten days. I do not know if my interpretation of what that meant and the police's interpretation was the same, but I just prayed to get home without finding out. I read and re-read that clause on my ticket and drove myself to work for the ten days. After that, the public bus and I became well acquainted. I knew what was sure to come with all the research I had done on the internet, so I sold my car right away.

I got a call from my insurance company about the incident and they wanted to know if I intended to put a claim in for the damage to my car. I told them there was none to my car. I recorded the agent's number and the case number assigned to me. I phoned five times afterward to inquire what had happened and in all cases I did not get any answer. I left detailed messages the first couple of times but since I never got a call in return I decided that the case from the taxi car owner must have been dropped. There was even a question of the type of vehicle I supposedly hit, the police had said it was a taxi and the insurance man called it limousine. Anyway I sold my car to a friend for much less than it was worth. I hurriedly sold it because I could not drive it anyway and at my new apartment I would have to pay for a special permit to park it on the city street. I no longer wanted to pay insurance, registration, or parking costs. I have a picture of the car the day I sold it on my bookshelf along with the classic Mustang I owned prior.

It took me a long time to get over the loss of my car. It was not the loss of driving since I adjusted to that easily. My place and my job were on the bus line, no problem there. I saved a lot of money too. God knew what He was doing. I just love camping road trips. I hope to take them again.

Efficient as ever, I wanted to get the entire drama over with a.s.a.p., so I contacted a lawyer right away. Low on money, I was assigned a public defender. She was available, helpful, and frank with me. At my first appointment in her office, I watched the police side-of-the-road video of myself trying to submit to the sobriety test. It was as entertaining as anything I had seen on the cop reality shows. Strangely, as my lawyer thought it was horribly incriminating, I did not think it was too bad. I had remained on my feet the whole time. I had been used to falling down a lot.

Before I left her office she asked me if I had ever thought about attending Alcoholics Anonymous (AA). I had heard of the group but did not know anything about it. She thought the judge might like it if I went to some meetings. In the end, she did not even bring the fact up to the judge. She suggested I make three meetings a week. Wow, I worked full-time and attended college full-time; I did not like this idea one bit. I told her I would try, I took the documents she gave me and left. On the way home I decided that I was in deep trouble and would follow my lawyer's advice to the "t".

I had trouble finding a meeting at first but once I did I was all set. I found meetings all over my neighborhood and forced attendance. The first few places I went to I felt totally out of place. These people were alcoholics, I did not relate at all. Thankfully, I did not give up but kept trying new places on the where and when list. I found some better places where the people were clean, well groomed, had jobs, and were educated. I felt better about these alcoholics and found a home. I urge anyone that has my initial experience to keep looking; there are meetings you will relate to somewhere. I find a lot of things about AA challenging to my faith. This is a very personal road and AA actually reminded me that I was a Christian and to start glorifying God like I should. The program is a bit too tolerant for me but it does tend to help people stay sober when all else has failed. Some may say that tolerance is a good thing, right? In some things of course it is like tolerating a crying child, but not if it turns people from their firm convictions to appease others. There is a saying that goes something like this. "If you do not stand for something, you will fall for anything."

I knew I should stop enjoying alcohol if trouble was going to follow me around when I did. A true statement I have learned goes like this, "I have not gotten into trouble every time I drank, but I had been drinking every time I got into trouble." True story. I vowed to quit and I did. The night of that arrest was my last drink and I have not desired one since. That is my God taking care of me. The stupid fun may be over but life is more than stupid fun. It is about real fun and responsibility and accountability to God. The horror of realizing I had been driving my car around the city nearly unconscious was my 'bottom'. This makes me a very fortunate person when compared to others. I started attending AA regularly and besides re-committing to God, I met some nice people. Some whacked people too I am afraid, but that comes with the territory.

My first court appearance was very brief. We basically just got a reprieve until I finished my semester. I had nearly two months of freedom to prepare mentally for the adventure. I counted down the days as if I were taking a camping trip. In the end, I noticed it was similar in some ways.

Chapter Four

I nervously laughed when people told me that I may have to serve jail time for this second offense. Denial has gotten me a long way in temporary peace of mind. It is not so bad to be positive and only face facts when it is sure, right? The punishment was multi-faceted again. The monetary fine was substantially greater than the first as was almost everything else. The cost of the fine was about $2600. I did not panic since I had the money to pay. I opted; however, to work much of it off. I did so at an animal rescue shelter. I had the time of my life there for a few weeks. The manager thought I was such a benefit to the shelter that he offered me a paid position. I was glad but the pay was lousy and I did not need a job just then. The work was very physical but the interaction with the dogs and cats made it tolerable. I grew tired after a while though and gave a notice, only to pay the remaining cost of the fine in cash.

I learned invaluable information from the shelter to file away. It had been in my mind for some time to open a dog shelter/boarding kennel of my own. The time serving gave me great ideas and addressed issues I would not have considered without the experience. Community service was not assigned to me this time but as mentioned I did it to reduce my fine. The probation was the same, one year. I could not end early because I was now such a notorious criminal that I could not be trusted. The price had increased $5 per visit also. Of course, I had to submit to five urine tests during the year at an additional cost. I was advised (non-negotiable) to take twenty-two weeks of substance abuse counseling. The classes were actually fun (except another weekly fee) but I hung my head low when the woman that ran the organization saw me. When I got released from her care less than two years prior, I assured her up and down that she would not see me again.

Used to the best intended sediments at that stage, she smiled and offered me encouragement. In sad truth, most clients do return.

The class was a mix of age groups, gender, race, and criminal experience. We played games, watched movies, completed homework, and shared hope one with another. I offered the hope of reliance on Christ and the benefit of AA. Some whole-heartedly backed me up while others scowled. Sadly, one of the clients that attended my class routinely arrived to class late and really reeked of liquor. The counselor was onto him I think because he asked him all the while if he was alright. He was not. I could barely stand the smell of him without throwing up. Over my time in counseling my sobriety time built up. I do not want to endure the shame of facing the ever-patient woman counselor again. That would be the least of my worries if I got arrested for DUI again, I would be a felon. That would mean that my life was a failure and game over. No proper job for me. God and my daddy would be very disappointed.

I lost my license for five years. Time and again, I find myself singing to myself that old Joe Walsh song that had lyrics saying, "I lost my license, now I don't drive." That's me. I would be eligible for a hardship license again but the cost is too prohibitive. I will not be driving anytime soon. I sold my car almost immediately to avoid paying further insurance on a vehicle that I could not drive. Storing it would have been too expensive. Oh, did I fail to mention the required punishment of the ignition interlock device? It would be necessary for me to install and maintain the unit for two years whether I got a hardship license or whether I waited the five years. So in effect, it is really going to turn into a seven year ordeal.

To buy another car, buy sky-rocketed insurance premiums, buy the license, and pay for the install and monthly charge of calibration on the device will be too much for this gal especially when I have to support myself and pay a steep student loan. I have not driven for so long already, it is no huge deal. I like my Trek bicycle. I am very environmentally friendly. I may never have a car again. Strangely, having a license is more valuable than the car. Above having to actually travel from one place to another, having a license is helpful for applications. I had no idea how many jobs require an applicant to have a driver's license when they surely will not be driving on the job. I think this may be a phenomenon of Florida because such a percentage of the people are criminal types here that the employers want to weed them out quickly. It sends a red flag if you are an adult no matter how your resume looks if you do not have a driver's license. This is quite a problem which leaves me in a bind. I do not even drink anymore.

The punishment continues. An unexpected cost of my crime is that having a DUI (even one) will keep me from traveling to the extent that I am used to. This loss of freedom is a blow. Canada will not allow U.S. citizens into their country with the conviction. Like me at first, most people do not believe it when I tell them that. I have done my research, however, and there will be no trips to Toronto for me. Apparently a special application can be presented that will cost a couple of hundred dollars that must be ready before the visit. Also proof of rehabilitation must be shown. I wonder what proof they accept. Would my DUI repeat offender substance abuse class completion diploma count? This must be the worst collateral damage to my life from the crime. I love travel and am most ashamed that I have shot myself in the foot again in this most important regard. Canada is one of the most beautiful countries. The photographs and notes I have from prior trips will have to hold me over until I get extra money to submit to this application process. I suppose this situation will also put the skids on my thoughts of working for the airline industry again.

Dear reader, do you get the message? Don't drink and drive. Besides all the selfish reasons, someone may get hurt or killed. I thank God often that I did not hurt anyone. He is giving me the chance to redeem myself; I do not want to fail. A good thing is that when I sold my car I had enough money left after paying off my loan to buy new furniture. There is always a bright side.

Once while sitting at the desk of my probation officer, I glanced at her wall décor. A list of punishments for the DUI crime in other countries and states was comforting. In a country in Central America, punishment is to be shot by firing squad at the first offence. I wonder if this is actually enforced. In Arizona, a DUI criminal must have a special pink identifying plate. That is so much worse than my orange impound sticker, which I did not have to suffer the second time even if I had not sold Genna (my car's name). I had just bought her a Daytona 500 license plate wrap-around a week before. Ironically, I drove across the state with a friend in my car and had nothing to drink since I knew I had to drive. There are times when I would be smart. Exactly one week later, game over.

The DUI safety course nearly doubled in price for the repeat offence. This class was also enjoyable. A very grim thing happened afterward. In my class was a good looking young man that also had two DUI offenses. I loved staring at him as he paid no attention to what was taught. Since I spend so much time staring at him, I probably could have learned more also. I learned that within a couple of months of gaining his completion certificate that he again got a DUI. He was only twenty-two, what a mess. Yes, not drinking at all is the safest way to avoid another DUI, falling down stairs, or flirting with men inappropriately.

A jail stay was in my future. I could moan and feel sorry for myself or take my medicine and learn from the experience. Since I am on the subject of medicine...

Part Three- County Jail

Chapter Five

... I naively tried to prepare for my month long stay by counting out enough aspirins to last me. Years earlier I had been prescribed 650 milligrams of aspirin a day to take for the rest of my life. This was to act as a blood thinner to keep any problems from the stroke I had suffered at bay. I packed them (and the written doctor's prescription) into my purse with cash, my passport, and house keys. I heard that I would be able to buy small things from a commissary and that I would be charged a booking fee. I thought this preparation would make me seem responsible. I would talk to someone important about my medicine; I packed the coated kind that I preferred.

I boarded the city bus to arrive at the courthouse at 9:00am; I didn't know what I was doing. I pulled the cord to get out and most of the rest of the bus got ready to disembark too, of course. The county complex was the major destination of this particular bus line. In a hurry to rise I dropped the bag of cheesy chex-mix onto the seat and my purse fell on it. Smooch, it left a crushed orange mess on the seat. All rules were made for a reason. Now I knew and had sympathy for the no eating on the bus rule. I would have cleaned it up any other time, really. So I looked down at it, glanced out the bus window at the county building growing bigger, I had to get out. I saw the disapproval in the faces of the passengers that remained on the bus. I felt guilty; I was a criminal.

I went through the metal detector quickly with my demure purse having consciously changed from my usual one for the occasion. The previous time I came through the line, my purse set off the detector. My bag was stuffed and the officer glanced in and then told me to dump it. Into the grey bin went the usual girly things plus about five dollars in change. It caused quite a racket and I was embarrassed. I then held up the line putting it all away. I did not know I would be subject to a metal detector screening.

After finding courtroom seventeen, I sat on a too-tiny ledge waiting for action. Other people started to arrive and I glimpsed my public defender talking to another one of her clients. Attractive men and women in fancy suits walked this way and that way amongst the many criminals. At this point, whether guilty or not, most of these people that gazed around the room waiting for the sessions to begin were dressed like thugs. They were not raised like I was. I learned early to dress properly and fitting to an occasion. Appearing before a judge in a court of law demanded demure dress and an air of respect.

A scripture series I happened upon while working on this paragraph struck me as fitting if not severe. The notion is the same. "And when the king came in to see the guests, he saw there a man which had not on a wedding garment. [11] And he saith unto him, Friend, how camest thou hither not having a wedding garment? And he was speechless.[12] Then said the king to the servants, Bind him hand and foot, and take him into outer darkness; there shall be weeping and gnashing of teeth[13]" (Matthew 22:11-13 KJV). The lesson, one should really dress for the occasion.

Most did not receive this memo. Women wore plunging necklines and hula-hoop sized earrings. The men wore inappropriate clothes as well but they were trumped in disrespect by the hoochy women. And remember this appointment was at nine in the morning. People's cell phone even rang during the session. Times had changed. This level of disrespect for the court was a foreshadowing of the experience I had once locked inside. This was an early indication that I was out of my element.

This is not to say the [whole] lot looked like a low-class lounge. I spied a few circumstances where a nervous mother that wanted desperately to change her child's path had forced them to dress correctly and held onto their arms for dear life. It was as if she did not want her child around these other types. I felt the mother's pain; I did not want to be around them either. This reinforced my decision about why I never wanted to become a parent. Too much uncertainty about what your child will turn into. These concerned women gave me hope and I felt gratitude toward my own upbringing. My parents were very strict and kept a close eye on us. In the modern world with single parents and everyone having to work tons of hours just to get by, it is almost impossible to keep your child from shifty influences.

In the middle of my judgment of the clothing and attitudes of those around me, I started to notice confusion in the hallway. As it turned out, one of the judges was not going to make it so the sessions had to get consolidated. This new snag made me nervous. I feared that my paperwork would get lost or confused with someone else's. As the group was ushered into the very tiny seating area of the courtroom, I saw my public defender paying attention to a lot of other criminals and ignoring me. While I liked her a lot, I was not impressed with her own appearance before the judge. Her long (to the waist) hair was hanging free and wild. I would have hoped her to have secured it into a demure bun for my case. Didn't she know that my life is being altered and I needed assurance and respectability from her? Finally she put her head in and summoned me into the hall. I was beginning to think she had forgotten about my case. As a public defender, I could tell that she was overworked but doing her best. We talked for a moment and she reminded me that this was it. I would be taken directly from this courtroom into custody for my "vacation." I phoned her afterward which she may have thought was unorthodox but I wanted to. I thanked her for helping me and for introducing me to AA.

Proceedings began. I witnessed a few cases before I was called. I got the impression that these other defendants were trying anything they could to get out of their just punishment and I heard many absurd excuses for irresponsibility. My air of superiority was heightened and compassion was in short supply. I understood completely why law enforcement agents at all levels lose their patience. I tried to talk myself into believing that this courtroom must be an exception. Maybe it is the neighborhood. Unfortunately, this is where all the criminals come from all the neighborhoods in the whole county. I forgot where I was and started to think that these people were a representation of the public at large. For some reason, I was feeling very philosophical. It must have been because I was being forced to look at the problems of society of which I had accidentally joined. I did not like it one bit, but I did not even leave the bright clean courthouse yet.

My turn came. I was embarrassed. I agreed to everything the judge said and listened intently when he scolded me about any further infractions along the same lines being a felony. This notion terrified me. How in blazes does a Christian, from a disciplined and loving home end up getting scolded by a man with a black robe and a gavel? Freak out. God wanted me back and he was getting me. It is apropos that I believe in the Bible verse that states that "all things work together for good for those that love God." I certainly have always loved him and now he was fixing to show me some tough love to get my attention. My ears and eyes were open.

The bailiff escorted me to the left-hand side of the room behind one of those half-swinging doors. Then he and another man fingerprinted me right in front of everyone else in the room. I took my medicine (shame) but I did not like it. Wake-up call number one, (two, I don't know) came right on the other side of the edge door. The calm conservatively decorated courtroom with the judge raised up presiding over the rest of the room was attached like a Siamese twin to the holding area for criminal processing. I gave up my jewelry and my tiny purse with my tiny stuff in it. I had hoped to be able to keep my medic alert necklace on because it was important. I learned that it was important only to me. The gloved officer bagged all my stuff. He also scolded me for having tablets in a container that was not labeled for the exact contents. Rowdy male inmates yelled at me and proffered gross gestures. I had been expecting just a walk down a nice transitional hallway to somewhere else.

I asked these officers about the money I had brought and my medicine. They would store the cash in some account for me to spend against at the commissary. I did not get any answers about my carefully planned out medicine. After a few more technicalities, the shorter of the two men handcuffed me and locked me in a room with a cinderblock partition in front of the simple toilet. Time did not seem to matter to me since I wasn't going anywhere for a while. I laid back and stared at the ceiling above my head and the upper portions of the cinderblock walls. I traced every edge repeatedly with my eyes, and prayed. Jingling keys woke me from my relaxation. I pulled up my body to look at a woman of about sixty placed in a room a few cells from me. I wondered what she had done to enter this palace.

It seemed that the officers were efficiency masters, I was surprised by that. We did not wait long at all when we got cuffed together and were made to wait in a dark hallway across from the boys. They seemed globally shorter than average. They were polite to both me and the other woman. I am sure the patrolling police with weapons kept them docile. I think the reality of it was that neither of the women waiting with them was under forty and they saw us as older people. There were only two of us being processed with probably twenty males.

The Sally Port was fun. The partitioned van had three sections. The name and the paint job made me feel like this was Disneyland. Obviously, I was eccentrically trying to be as positive as possible. Later I noticed that the ride was rough enough to hurt my back. It seems that these Sally Ports are a regular thing and the name is generic for these type of vans whether for the police, the military or others. They are a mystery to me and I still don't know who all uses them and why they are called by such a lively title. Efficiency was still the name of the game. A hard blue bench seat was revealed when the door was opened and we were gestured in. The officer gave the woman his hand for guidance. I always have liked them (the police- belief it or not). They are generally polite unless provoked. It is strange that I had dated policemen in the past and now I was in official custody not play custody.

In the other side of this container on wheels, two male inmates sat. One of them politely smiled at us while the thinner talked to us respectfully. I was impressed with the unexpected respect from these two young men. As was revealed earlier, I judge people harshly and I thought they would talk filth to us or something. I had no idea what they had done of course. They might not even be real criminals, just like me.

The process of loading us from the van was interesting. Giant gates rose to let the van drive through and another set were closed in front of the van soon to be caged in. Only once had I seen this far inside of a jail. It was twenty years ago when a friend was jailed for protesting about abortion. He was effective; he converted me. When the doors were opened, an assembly line of counters and officers in green tones bagged clothing, shoes, and all the things they took behind the comfortable courtroom. These were mostly women and they had foul attitudes. That was strange compared with the male guards that were so perfect up until I wanted to curse a balding, egomaniac later in my stay.

Again, I tried to explain my need for my aspirin and asked about my money. I was ignored. I learned later that even though I saw no sign of recognition when I stated my concerns, they had heard me. This callous treatment must be a psychological technique to reinforce the proper relationship between the comers and stayers and the uniforms that would be home for dinner (maybe a movie tonight, Jerome)?

Both sexes sat in a waiting area. I did not know about the indignity I was soon to suffer. Two stern females motioned me into a private room where I undressed and worse. I bet the reader knows what I mean. It was unpleasant. I knew some criminals had to get strip-searched but surely not me. I was only arrested for having too much fun and I have always been quite docile. I was no criminal that planned on breaking any laws, strange how my justifications work. It is true though, there are people that set out to do wrong and those that do wrong accidentally, I am definitely of the latter type of criminal. At least it was clear to me that the two female officers that took me into that tiny room were not enjoying what they had to do.

I did notice that many other people still had their own shoes on their feet. The black rubber flops the woman assigned me looked very fashionable with my socks. I could not figure out what the criteria could be for deciding who gets to keep their own shoes. Why was I separated from my shoes? Already, my attitude was turning south. It was not long when the woman and I were placed in a room with a see-thru top and dull light green painted lower halves. The older woman looked depressed. I thought I got her name in the Sally Port but I could be dreaming. I kind of wanted to talk to her but what is appropriate? I was not going to ask her any personal questions. What do you do or do you have any grandchildren? Not right now. I hoped to kind of will her some encouragement and prayed for her situation. Soon we were joined by a stocky woman that was flapping her arms at the assembly line officers and yelling expletives. I secretly willed her to just shut up. When we left that area, we were led down a hall. The third woman went missing, at least I never saw her again.

Another Sally Port ride took us somewhere else. Sad companion and I peeked out the front window of the van trying to see where we were going with the heads of the police officers bobbing in front of us. We did not speak to each other. When the door opened it was like a little house in front of us. This is not any jail building that I have ever seen before. I learned later that this is what was called a mini. I was assigned to mini 2- pod 6. This information would have been vital if I planned on corresponding with outsiders. I did not. I told my friends, co-workers, and neighbors that I would call them in a month. I already started to consider the free as outsiders.

The yard was muddy but welcoming with trees and grass. I later noticed the height of the fence that corralled in the area about ten feet on either side of the walk of shame pavement. Inside we were separated and I never saw that woman again either. I never even noticed her in the cafeteria. Since she was driven to the same unit and brought inside with me, I should have seen her in the cafeteria at least. It seems that as soon as we walked through that front door that she disappeared. It was just me and the abrupt blonde officer behind the window until a trusted inmate 'helper' arrived from space to settle me in.

Inside this small house, six dormitory-type rooms called pods were designed as home to criminals at any stage in their careers. The glass in front was doors and windows tinted a slate grey. A pretty blond officer with an adolescent hair bow oversaw me while I signed into the building. A thin black woman appeared with white sneakers, an orange suit, and led me down a hall to the restroom; I had to have my things bagged again. Where were the guards? So far this place just looked like a regular house.

I was in the charge of this friendly, humming black woman. She fed me a beefy disc with sauce and rice, a cookie as bland as a matzo ball, and delicious apple juice. I already liked this food appearing before me. This benefit of jail is underrated. I saved a fortune on food during my stay. My charge was only six dollars altogether. It was the booking fee. The cafeteria had horizontal windows way above my head. Row after row of long tables had orange plastic chairs lining the flat surfaces like sentinels. On the opposite side of the room from the tables and chairs was the kitchen. Soon, walking along that wall three times each day with its open counter sustainers (meals) would become the highlight of my days.

The food was good. I had been fed the evening leftovers. It was light outside when I entered. I would soon be getting used to one of the biggest threats to my harmony during the next weeks. I guess meal times are not important when there is no time. I was not going anywhere-anytime soon. Nevertheless, the three-thirty breakfasts and four-ish dinners really had me confused. It must be another psychological technique no doubt. The meals came to be the things that I looked forward to. I had no qualms about the food, was shocked at the level of complaining from the other inmates, and was grateful. In real life, I always thought a lot about food because it took up so much of my budget. I think I succeeded in frugality but this eating for free for a month had my vote. Besides, the food was really good.

    A holler came from around the corner, it was a cue to finish eating and head to the next step of assimilation. The black woman fed me and was polite to me but did not give me any information. It must be learn as you go. I chose a mat off the floor and a bundle of linen (rolled blanket, sheet, case, wash cloth and towel) and felt suddenly abandoned in the hallway alone. I followed the curve until I was facing the reception window again. The short, blond officer behind the window wanted nothing to do with my questions. She just pointed to her right and I walked that way. It is sad that the officers all seemed to think that all of the inmates were bad people. They did not seem to understand the tiny mistakes that place genuinely good people in this temporary condition. Ask the monitor was all she would say. What did she mean? Why couldn't she just answer my simple questions? I later learned that most of the inmates there see jail and a life of crime as a permanent condition. Hope was scarce in the pod I soon joined.

Chapter Six

Still surprised by the bad treatment from the blonde woman, I dragged my green vinyl stuffed mattress behind me. The scene that met me was an instant delight. The bunk beds with girls of all colors and sizes moving around the room in small cliques reminded me of the many years spent sleeping in youth hostels (not quite as entertaining as the time in New Zealand when I awoke to two British chaps changing their clothes in my view). My mind was taking this vacation thing to its height. I tend to accept bad things well and the weeks I had to prepare for this day had me ready to start with the most positive attitude possible. By the end of my stay, I had drawn a calendar on my notepad and x'ed out each new day. At that point, I had enough. On my last few days, visions of my nearing release must have been fogging my mind, because I did not cross of the days of June 1st or 2nd on my noted calendar.

A group of girls moved forward to welcome me and soon I realized that the leader of this party was Trish. She was the current acting monitor of this pod- pod #6. Before this moment I had envisioned sharing a cell with one or just a few other women. I thought it would be quiet and solemn. There was little quiet and no solemnness. It was like a crazy, out of control slumber party.

Walking further into my pod, I found that this room had 42 beds. Three were currently empty and I picked a top bunk nearer the shower room/toilets. The green mattress fit the metal frame perfectly. I thought I heard a few people commenting that my mattress had a build in pillow. There were two types and I had grabbed the first one I saw. I hoped that something as petty as this would not put up a wall between me and my new roommates. I had a pancake pillow also but the built in one would add comfort possibly causing derision between me and some unreasonable types. I laid the sheet and blanket on the way I typically would prepare a bunk when traveling. Over my shoulder, a couple of the girls told me to do it differently. I crawled onto my nest and intended to mind my own business. "No, it's fine," I said. The girls were persistent that I get down and let them teach me the "correct" way to make up the bunk in county jail. I came to appreciate the tips I learned from these girls and how creative people get when they have time and need on their hands.

Obediently, I swung my legs down and tried to appear graceful as I jumped to the cold, speckled floor. I watched fascinated as two girls worked together to tightly tie the sheets around the ends of the mattress. Once I considered why it was done this way, I thought maybe it was because the people below would not tolerate edges of bedding hanging into their areas. I suppose that the practice helped to keep the feet warm too. I said, "Yeah that's good. I'm sorry. I'm just starting." One of them replied, "I know that's right." This phrase must have been some slang in circles other than mine. I had never heard it before. All the girls used it and soon I was saying it for all circumstances also. When I was free and living life again and I would hear a person around town say, "I know that's right," I would fondly thing of my pod-mates.

Back up in my bunk, I leaned against the wall observing the room. From the time I arrived time had little meaning to me. The meal times puzzled me but I cared less about time. I had nothing pressing so I just did hygiene care, slept, read, or wrote whenever I felt like it and went to eat when called. It was all simple and agreeable. While chilling (pun intended) I soon noticed that just feet above my head was the grate in the ceiling blowing cold air right on me. I had been warned about the frigid temperatures I would face. Strangely, fighting the uncomfortable cold was the worst memory from my stay.

No one paid any attention to me once I settled onto my bunk. I started remembering things I needed to consider such as: I need books, how do I tell someone about my medicine needs, what about this commissary? I was anxious to learn the routine and what to expect. I would have to beg information from these girls. I studied the room. The inner corner had glass windows and the officers glanced in every once in a while. I could only see the door if I kneeled up on my bunk. A TV was hanging from the ceiling above a short bookshelf. A cork board with notices had a ledge where I saw girls place papers. I learned that this was the communication zone between the officers and the inmates. Outgoing mail, form 62s going out and signed; acknowledged 62s (sometimes with notes- eg.-class granted) were traded from this ledge. When incoming mail arrived, an officer would come in, call out names, and throw the letters on a table. The rest of the front part of the room was filled with round tables and the bunks where trouble girls slept so the officers could watch them closely. This was a joke since they never stayed in their area. Nighttime was when the guards had concern for surveillance on these girls but it was laughable. Supposedly the sexually active lesbians were forced to bunk in the front to keep them from any shenanigans.

It was evening now and girls were playing board games, writing on pads, staring (or yelling) at the person on the pay-phone willing the user to get off, or sitting staring at the TV. Often they burst out with comments as if the people on the screen could hear them. I have done that plenty in my own living room during political talks or sports but to see women randomly yelling at the TV and each other in "public" was alarming. This room full of animated women acting like they were at a slumber party was entertaining.

The bookshelf was lame with mostly romance novels lining two shelves with games on the bottom. I caught Trish's attention and tried to find out if I could get a hold of any books other than these. I would walk over to this shelf often willing a decent title to show up. I bet that I was the only person ever to read *The Detention and Correction Bureau's Inmate Handbook* from cover to cover. I studied the library section on page ten. This was a ruse to tease book addicts. When I inquired many times, I was laughed at or told I was dreaming. But there it was outlined in the official handbook. Trish gave me a couple of form 62s that she pulled from a blue folder under her pillow. The forms came with no verbal help from Trish. My first 62 was a request for any non-fiction books. No response.

I learned to observe. Blessedly, I found a science book on the shelf and took it to my bunk like a treasure. On my bunk, I read the small print on the form 62. I was to write any requests or needs to the officers via these forms. They were what the others had been placing on the board ledge. I learned that this system was untrustworthy. At least, I found that many notes were ignored by the officers that picked them up. I wondered if they just tossed them into the trash. Of the many notes I wrote, the only ones answered were for a Bible from the chaplain, and the request to go to AA and self-defeating behavior meetings. I did not sign up for church services because the denomination choices did not thrill me and basic non- denomination Bible study was not an option.

In a setting like the county jail, I was surprised at the small opportunity to go to AA meetings. The help-groups only met most often twice a week. Some of the offerings that I found out about from the cork bulletin board included many different faith meetings, anger-management, self-defeating behavior, and AA/NA. Meals were served in a military fashion. The girls would have benefited from even more military-style treatment. The county probably feared that someone may cry that their rights had been violated. Sad stuff, discipline needed to be taught to these girl aggressively. They were not getting it in jail and would not get it in their worlds either. I tried to force my philosophical side to take a vacation while I was on 'vacation' but the monster kept surfacing.

Women's sneakers, flops, and personal shoes were strewn all over the area under the bunks pushed against plastic bins assigned to the inmates that were in the bunks above. My bin so far had a tiny toothpaste, toothbrush, shampoo/soap and I would later add a commissary black dick-tracy comb. I should have rented out space in my bin. I could have gotten extra candy bars. I already had my flops under my pillow and the white sneakers placed in the groove of metal closest to the wall where I lay. Suspicion had ahold of my mind. I never had a healthy trust of other women anyway, men seem easier to interact with and get a take on. I concluded that only God and I could be trusted in this group. Watching the friction between the girls, the language they used, their tattoos, and the broad degradation of the pod culture put me in self-protective mode. I said little or nothing but observed everything.

I saw women getting things out of their bins and I wondered if they were staying for a year. Most people had stores of junk food and so many personal care items I think they forgot they were in jail. When I got my hands on a commissary sheet the next day, the offerings included music systems (what- is this really happening- in jail), almost any junk food a person could crave, and brand name deodorant and shampoo. It did not seem to me that these choices were appropriate. I studied it many times trying to decide what to spend my few dollars allotment on besides the non-negotiable candy bars. The clothes were very cheap but I was cheaper. If I ventured to spend the money, I could have stayed nice and toasty warm.

The inmates did not seem to suffer any punishment. They might have been in an apartment with roommates. I figured out that the county is very interested in earning a profit enabling the girl's materialism and shallowness. In no regard was any attempt made to turn these girls from the wrong path they were blazing that I could discern. Indeed, as I eavesdropped on the conversations of those near my bunk, my hope for them got less and less each day. They spoke of the crimes they had done, the ones their friends were doing right now, and how they were anxious to get released so that they could continue doing the things that put them in the situation in the first place. Most had come to peace with the horrible idea that this would be their life-cycle. Gratitude fell over me since I trusted in God to carry me through this ordeal and that once I got free I would continue to move forward in life and act responsibly in society. I was raised properly and I would have to make this disappointment up to my father.

I had a natural landscape science book to browse and I had found an AA big blue book. I stayed in my bunk observing and listening until lights out. I realized on the first night that about half of the girls did not care an iota that the others in the room may want to sleep. Choosing a bunk in the back was a mistake. I was closest to the restrooms with the lights glaring all night and since the glass windows were at the other end of the pod, the girls danced-sang-fought all night long. Only a couple of times while I was there did an officer enter the room to investigate the noise. Of course as soon as the doors opened, everyone was an angel pretending to sleep.

The nighttime Shangri-La was a giant irritation during my stay. It took hard prayer to hold my scolding tongue. Other, braver girls would protest but that would lead to a certain fight. The situation caused resentment since the lights came on and the call to breakfast would be raised at 3:30am. It was to breakfast like a zombie many mornings having had no sleep at all. Chaos ruled at first call. Everyone rushed to the restroom and raced and pushed in an attempt to be close to the door when it opened. It would mean eating earlier. The smallest competitions between the girls were invented out of nothing and would often lead to irrational arguments. The group at large had serious socialization issues. Some girls even took the time in the morning at breakfast to do up their hair and add make-up. I realized that since there were six pods in this building, there was a chance of seeing a friend that was in another pod. Meals were socialization events. I took to introversion well and the isolation from the outside didn't bother me. I did not make any calls while I was there, and I did not have any visitors. I did start to converse with the girls and found them individually to be nice enough.

I had made an enemy of the girl living in the bunk below me. She let me hear it when I swung my legs over the edge of my bunk and jumped to the floor. I did not even notice that my spider legs had been in her face and I nearly kicked her in the head whenever I sprung from the top. I did not realize she and her friends (as happened in all the bottom bunks I later noticed) were making the bunk into a fort. With so many girls crowded onto a single bunk for chat, it was hard not to club someone on my way down.   A stone gripped my heart when she loudly yelled at me. To preserve my harmony, I came back from the toilet and meekly asked her forgiveness and promised to use the stairs from then on. Even then I always threw my head over the edge to check the situation before debunking. This probably did not endear me to her either. If she had been really nasty she would have picked a fight with me for getting into her business. Thankfully, she realized that I was just starting and had no idea about jail etiquette. I did not want any outstanding friction between myself and anyone. She seemed like one of the tougher girls in the pod, I wanted to get on her good side. Her name was Marty. It was a party on her bunk and all of the lower bunks all night and day. At least I did the right thing choosing the top. I get protective of my space as a trait and I would have had a harder time adjusting to being in jail if all the other girls thought my bunk was their bunk. I had a haven above the others and a great vantage point. I never once found another girl trying to cozy up onto my bunk. God provides small but important favors.

Before daylight at breakfast time I was educated about the unspoken rules. A person will try to wake up another with a shake if they did not hear the call or notice the lights on. If they roll over, they get no free food. I failed to wake up only once and gratefully was shaken by Ricky. I wanted all of my meals. The inmates were herded into the cafeteria to follow the outstretched arm of an officer to know where to sit once we went through the line receiving trays and drinks. It was amazing but understandable to consider the regimentation of meals. It was pleasantly militaristic, which I thought was good for the girls.

Still, many broke the rules by hiding food under their tops, taking plastic flatware hidden, and mouthing off. It was not long before I became a favorite of the cafeteria staff inmates. I was always grateful for the food and thanked them every time. I liked most everything that was served but if one of my favorites turned up I would be animated in my happiness. I have no idea why I love food so much. I was fed well growing up. It is still a mystery to me today since I struggle with holding food up as an idol. Gratefully, somehow I have always remained skinny.

The cafeteria was a bargaining place. Food was traded in every direction. I liked this because it often played in my favor. The bargaining started immediately since time was short. Portable foods were handed down rows and to other tables. Trays raised high to a friend would mean a quick scrape off of one plate to another for messy things. The officers were amazingly tolerant of this. It was understood that all milk would be handed to Ricky since she was expecting soon. She also had two mattresses on her bunk. I liked her, she seemed like she wanted to take the straight road now for the sake of her baby. When she spoke on the phone with or got letters from her boyfriend though, I felt sadness creeping in. Ricky would have to be mature for both of them. I don't know where she is but I pray she no longer hangs with a rough crowd and is creating a responsible example for her child and finding joy for herself. The day she left was celebration and happiness to her from everyone.

It took me a long time to figure out what the hot brown coffee-stuff served to us in the morning really was. The server inmates verbally said, "Do you want coffee?" It was the strangest coffee I had ever tried. It tasted healthy (whatever that means) so I just kept ordering it. This mystery coffee and milk were served only at breakfast and otherwise we got water from a square cooler or juice (more like tang or high C- but yummy) from a twin cooler. We had to eat like fiends to finish before we were told our time was up. Then ready or not, the tray was dumped and the cups emptied into the trash. The officers oversaw the trash can operation. Gratefully full after meals, I arranged my pillow against the wall to keep my face from lying against the cold, dirty wall and snoozed long.

I found my bed to be plenty comfortable but having more blankets would have been a dream come true. I tried folding the blanket the short way to cover more of my girth but then my giant feet were cold. The opposite method meant I had to try to stay real still or my flanks would stick out. I shivered plenty while curling up into a ball to stay warm. When the lights flashed a second time in the day, it was call to recreation. The whole time I was in jail, I only went out twice. They only allowed a handful of girls from each of the pods to go outside. I stayed in my bunk through the first fresh air opportunity. If I had known how rare the chance came, I would have gone out to see the sky. After all, I had just arrived and wanted to stay on these women/girls good sides. I found that they have heightened sensitivity and low tolerance. I made it out the next day. All I could think about was getting some paper and a pencil or something decent to read.

Shower time had to get timed well. With so many people in the pod, it was wise to keep one eye on who went in and out, so as to jump in an empty stall quickly. I admit I tarried in the shower because it was the only place to be hotly comfortable. A positive part of the shower situation was that it was impossible not to notice the other women's physiques. I decided mine was decent enough. The room had three showers. About halfway through my stay one of the stalls started to back up and would not drain properly. This added to the mystery of when to make a break for the shower room. Most would not go in there. Some would if they planned on being super quick. It made the girls even more discontented. At times I would encounter a girl preparing to shower at the same time as me and we would both stand undressed eyeing each other over the better shower stall. I always demurred because I was a greenhorn and a mighty cautious citizen (from John Wayne's- *Angel and the Bad Man*).

The strangest thing was common in the showers. One of the women was tying a maxi pad somehow around the shower nozzle. What the purpose of that was, I will never know. Of course, she left it in place when she was done-dirty wench. Hot water was always available in the showers. I saw this as a real surprise and a blessing. The cold would have been unbearable if I could not escape into the hot haven once a day. Showers were not limited so the girls could go as often as they wanted. It was like a field trip so I only went once a day. I mean, hope the towel is dry, gather the soap, and watch and wait. It was a lot of work compared to anything else I was doing. We only had one towel which we could change out twice a week. They took forever to dry in the cold rooms and we could not hang them properly.

The restroom had three toilets lined against the wall with three urinals mounted to the opposite wall. The pod building was a male holding center beforehand. The urinals became holding centers for extra toilet paper and maxi-pads. It was awkward but soon became bearable to pee or strain with other girls right there with you. This is something I could have lived forever and not experienced.

While leaning against the wall of my bunk, I noticed a woman walking paces back and forth. I admired her at first for holding to her exercise routine even in jail. That day she thought it was her turn to go to the yard for exercise and when denied, she acted out in defiance. She spoke to herself a lot and I can relate to that. Her name was Julia. By the end of my stay I thought she was spiteful, selfish, and uncooperative. You never know someone until you live with them for a while. Isn't that what the old adage says?

I could not bear the programs the girls chose. When there was a challenge to what channel to put on, I could not believe the shows they were fighting for. I hoped for some sports or news but it was soap operas and games shows. In the evenings, I saw *American Idol* frenzy.

Now that I was accepted in the room, I started concentrating on each girl. At times trying to think about what makes them think the way they do. I mostly felt like I was invisible in the room, just like a fly on the wall.

I did not confront anyone about anything (not yet) and they were good with that. There were girls with wedding rings on, a woman walking around swallowing sugar packets, and step right up twenty-four hour hair-braiding. After having a talk with a girl in a meeting about her ring, I found out that if the ring was too tight, you could keep it. One woman did not speak at all for my first two weeks and then let it all flow. That was Linda. The room was a study in group dynamics, psychology, and spiritual warfare.

The jail experience was a bleeding heart's dream. Any social worker, psychologist, or minister could stay busy forever just trying to fix these girls. This situation almost but not quite turned me into an altruist. That is nearly a dirty word to me, somewhat unfortunately I reckon. I wanted so bad to believe that the people that I met here would suddenly change their situations. The longer I remained; however, the more pessimistic I became. Only God Himself could make a difference here, and I prayed that He would. I know that prayer is powerful so I used that tool. He worked here as much as anywhere else through the mysterious channels he often enlists. It is admirable that the people that bring in meetings, the social workers, the clergy, and even the officers do what they do to so little acclaim and appreciation. It truly takes a selfless individual to try to make a difference in the lives of the inmates with seemingly so little hope. Faith must get them through. Even if they are often crabby and lose patience that must be understood given the territory. My hat is off to all of them. It is queer how I am talking again about the other inmates as if I am not one of them. My record proves that I am.

Lunch call at 10:30am? Well, I will need energy for all this sleeping I've been doing. The same march in for lunch-y food this time. After a while, I noticed a woman from a different pod that always came to meals with a pad and pencil. She was unmolested by the officers as she went around speaking to the other inmates while the meal was underway. She also had glasses on. Did any of the others have glasses or were they taken away as property (contraband)? I cannot remember anyone else wearing glasses. A few days of eavesdropping and I learned that this woman was a paralegal in outside life and was working on helping many girls with their cases. She even somehow had access to legal books. I felt slighted. If there were legal books in the building there must be other good non-fiction for me. I was jealous because she had books but mostly admired her for spending her free time helping the others. I hope she was helping the worthy and not the girls that were just acting like crybabies that did not want to accept their punishments.

As I will continue to repeat, I enjoyed the food a lot. Thoreau was right about the enjoyment a person can take in the simple things in life, a roof over the head, heat for the body, and food. I planned to get by with the three provided meals each day. The food the girls had stock-piled in the bins below their beds was often the cause of derision. Girls would write nasty letters to their boyfriends or parents for not putting enough money into the docket number account. Hearing them swear endlessly to the same effect on the phones was absurd. Some of these orders topped $100 each week. This was the mindset; I want it, you pay for it. Frugality has always been one of those traits I possess that are a blessing and a curse. Honesty is another one. I am brutally honest because if I am not, a little birdy will tell anyway. Of course, the more food a girl stocked in her bin, the more she was subject to begging or the threat of thievery. The begging bothered me infinitely.

I hoped to leave with some of my money left over. It took me a long time to budget my purchases that first commissary day. A pad and pencil was mandatory. Since I was freezing to death, I ordered a white t-shirt to wear under my orange frock. I noticed the other girls had written their names onto the collars. It proved to be a project getting a Sharpie marker from the officers for the task. All clothes that went to the laundry had to get marked: socks, underwear, t-shirts, and more. Since the marker was obviously needed, I do not know why one could not stay in the pod under the supervision of the monitor. It was contraband no doubt. The girls may have tried to get high by sniffing it, I reckon. I was smart to have heeded an important tip or two from my pre-jail inquiring. I came to court with three pairs of undies on, one over the other. I did the same with socks. It was a shame when the grouchy women officers that searched me in booking had taken my knee-highs. I had dreams of them holding in the heat against my skin. Everything was contraband in the pod.

I could keep reversing my undies and socks to the greatest hygienic benefit. My panty-liner scheme did not pan out. The officers did not miss a trick. Of course, by the end and too cheap to have bought any undies from the commissary, I took to washing my undies in the sink. I had to lay them flat on my bunk blanket to dry. The girls would have loved to see me try and hang them over the edge of my bunk. They looked for any silly reason to argue. No, I would not do anything that might raise the ire of these tough girls. There were enough daily unsavory happenings; I did not want to become what I hate.

So, one pad, one pencil, one white undershirt, peanut M&M's and a Three Musketeers Bar ended up as my first order. I got to order things from the red and white sheets twice a week. It was like an exam, be careful to fill in the entire circle of your choice in black pencil. I had already spent almost six dollars. I still had to wait for the stuff though. I ordered those same two candy bars on every commissary order. The candy was my only extra food to supplement the three shove and run meals. The others knew I only ordered this and I ate both treats within ten minutes of receiving them. This worked wonders to ward off beggars and hustlers. I had nothing that anyone else might want and they left me alone. I guarded my paper and pencil at all times. I wrote so much for entertainment that I am sure the others thought I was writing things about them. Often, I was. As far as I know, though, no one tried to spy on the notes while I was showering.

I started looking at publication's writing guidelines or editor's names every time I saw a newspaper or magazine. I hoped to expand on what my travel writing professor had taught me about marketing. *Readers Digest* was available to study as was the *Tampa Bay Times* and the *AAGrapevine.* I wrote down the editor's names, the publication's addresses, what kind of writing they would pay for, and helpful anecdotes from each. I copied a bullet list of advice from the *Reader's Digest* which was entitled, "Gladwell's Five Steps to Success." I wanted to memorize them and apply them. They are reproduced below for anyone else interested in success.

1. Find meaning and inspiration in your work.

2. Work hard.

3. Discover the relationship between reward and effort.

4. Seek out complex work to avoid boredom and repetition.

5. Be autonomous and control as much of your own destiny as possible.

These are sound words for anyone. I also learned that the same magazine would pay potentially $100 for funny jokes. Well over a year later I do not have anything funny to sell. I also wrote the beginning of my first book, *Will Travel with Consequences*, on my notepad. The words did not make it into the final cut. When my introverted writing time got boring, I observed and entered the room's atmosphere with my senses alert.

Mercedes was a jolly, beautiful girl. She was the first to reach out to me and invite me to borrow a couple of books she had in her bin. She sensed I was going out of my mind without something decent to read. Mercedes always looked great. She constantly changed her hairstyle, and put cosmetics on. It took me a long while to discover that it is true what you hear about these jails. I began to pay attention and learnt that the majority of these girls had girlfriends. Many of them held in other pods in this very building. This explains the care about appearances (absurd primping) among the girls at mealtime.

The girls got out of the room if they were prearranged in a group meeting. If so, officers would open the door and shout names or use the loudspeaker which was illegible. The girls only went to these meeting because they had arranged through code or something which ones they joined and their friends joined also. The topic of the class was irrevelent. They were not really interested in self-improvement. Most of the girls were too young to consider their future. One girl was eighteen but spoke and looked like a very young child. I was horrified after hearing her tell some others that she thought she was pregnant. I could not believe it. I did not know what kind of a man would have sexual relations with this girl that seemed so much like a child. My despair for the human condition grew and grew through simply observing the room.

Each day after lunch, rotations of girls were responsible for the cleaning of the pod. Worried that I would miss my turn and make the girls resent me, I constantly asked Trish when it would be my turn. She assured me my day would come but did not give a clue. I watched as other girls swept and mopped the floors, and wiped the tables and chairs. I know a special team of trusted inmates came in late at night to clean the toilets and showers. Like clockwork, it would be during those forty-five minutes when most of the girls had to use the toilet. Sometimes, they just wanted to chat. This happened to me so much that I mostly suffered by holding it in until they left. I used to clean for a living; even friendly people will be harsh if you get in their way.

The officers sometimes came randomly in at night and woe to those that were not at least sitting on their bunk. I held it a lot. There was a speaker in the room that I was told was two-way. In other words, we could hear them on the intercom and they could spy on the noise in the pod. I do not really believe this because they ignored the pitched noise volume almost every night. I think if the intercom was two-way like a baby monitor that they chose to turn it off while they did cross-word puzzles or watched shows. Word puzzles like cross-word would have been a great addition to the bookshelf offerings. Granted, the piece puzzles were better than nothing but the cross-words would force these girls to think. I do not think most of them were in the habit of applying their brain to anything. They acted on emotion and instinct.

I talked to God a lot. I knew He would take care of me in there. In a few days the Bible I ordered arrived from the chaplain. In order to get it into my hands, I had a personal interview with her. I sat alone with her in the cafeteria talking to her about The Lord. She deemed me fit to receive the Holy Book and we even prayed together. She was a 60ish woman with a grey bob and a loose white blouse with triangles on it. I felt comfortable with her and was grateful for her calling to work in the jail. She is obviously a better Christian than me. I tucked the Book under my arm and waved to the officer indicating that I was ready to return to the lion's den. It was a nice version. I have since passed it on to a friend and am saddened when I look at his desk and see it buried under his other more pressing work. Maybe he will open it someday.

The Recovery Bible broke down the chapters into sections and related verses and circumstances to how it parallels the traditional twelve step recovery (see Appendix E). Whether you are having a problem with alcohol, drugs, caffeine, food, gambling, or anything else that people hold up as idols, the same twelve steps if applied lead to recovery. I hid this carefully under my mattress in the corner. What really surprised me was that copies of the Bible were not crowding the bookshelf. Instead a special meeting was required to obtain a copy. I think one should be handed out to each inmate first thing. They will eventually pick it up out of boredom. I know Bibles are sold at the dollar stores for [a dollar]. Was this about not offending inmates of non-Judeo/ Christian faiths?

I also read the entire AA big blue book in about two days. I call the AA book the big blue book because I get insulted for Christ when people refer to it as the Big Book. To me, only the Bible is the Big Book. AA stresses finding a higher power and that is fine with me if it is the Christian Christ. The reader hopefully will forgive my typical Jesus Freak intolerance of other gods. The trouble is it accepts any other false god choice a person can fabricate as valid. Reading the big book is so stressed that it recommends a higher power but fails to point you to where to look to know Him. Instead of memorizing the big blue book and spending time reading it every day, I feast on His own words. The big blue book is a good book, but only as a supplement to the Word of God.

It was disappointing to hear dinner called at about 4:30pm. This would be the last time I would eat until 3:30am. Wow, I feel so spoiled by writing that sentence. Another idea of Thoreau's that I try to claim (mostly in philosophy only) is that one meal a day is adequate to sustain a person. We were fed plenty at each meal and the girls that complained were spoiled brats. That is surely the state of the new generation. I want to call them generation W. for What? Many of the girls had obligations each day. I felt relieved when the days wore on and I did not have to take on an assignment. I was content with my sleeping, reading, and note-taking. Some of the work the girls did included kitchen duty, cleaning offices, and sewing. I felt the pain of the girls that were called out early. It was a bummer to be in jail and still have to get up in the wee hours of the day to go to "work." This would have totally broken my adventure of a different kind vacation. The girls grumbled endlessly about their "jobs." I surmised that it must be a part of the plea they arranged. I did not understand the entire logistics of the matter and I hoped not to either. It was a true pity that these girls were known by the officers and each other. It was really their way of life. After dinner the girls watched shows (read American Idol), played games, or danced and sang around the room.

Chapter Seven

Lateasha, who slept in the top bunk directly across from me, was the rudest girl in the room after lights out. Nighttime unsettled me more than any other time. It was the ignorance of her and others that kept me restraining myself nightly from screaming at them at the top of my lungs. I would then have been a part of the problem and surely would have made new enemies. There was no rationality. The conservative, smart woman (I will include myself in that group) laid with their forearms over their ears (despite our flip-flop ear plugs) and our heads under the covers. Sleep was obviously a day time activity. It took me a long time to realize that the schedule was more in keeping with most of the girl's routine. I would say that most of the young girls that fussed so much did not have day jobs outside and that most of the crime they were guilty of occurred at night. They were just doing what they were used to and the rest of us should get with the program, right? I even harbored an idea of spending some of my commissary cash on a radio set. This went against my budgeting but I could have put the blessed ear buds on and listened to the music of my own choice instead of the girl's singing. And the songs they were singing were definitely not to my taste. White noise would have been my best friend at night. Loud white noise.

The music headphones that these spoiled young people wore blasted music beyond the ear buds. Even worse, the girls also had to sing along LOUDLY. Could it be that they were innocent and did not know how loud they were. I suppose this could be true but I already held judgments against them and the ability to give them the benefit of the doubt was waning. The girls ran around the room like animals in the subdued darkness. I loved it on the rare nights when the officers finally made an appearance to calm everyone down. The girls would carry on the exact same way once the door clicked shut behind them on their way out, but for the few minutes the enforcement presence was in the room at least, it was calm.

I waited for breakfast. Peanut butter and honey on bread with cereal and milk is the favorite. At the door with my cup in my hand, I waited to find out. Well, oatmeal is almost like cereal and the oranges are tiny, gloomy, but juicy. I could not complain. After a nap, I was lucky to get outside on this day. It was rather over-rated. Two officers escorted the group (about thirty from all pods) to a fenced-in area and corralled us in. The space was approximately one hundred-fifty feet by seventy-five feet. The lazy girls sat on picnic table benches and talked. Others walked laps around the perimeter, some jogged. Small cliques of girls formed in huddles. It was a very sad episode.

The contrast of the high fence with the people caged in against the vast sky and openness beyond that corral was depressing. It forced you to remember where you were. An exercise room with equipment like treadmills or stationery bikes would have been a dream. I am sure that the county budget did not include that type of luxury. I thought; however, that instead of an exercise room as a luxury, it would be a basic human need almost to the tune of food. Forty girls in one room with no outlet most days could not be good for anything. I suppose the decision makers thought that giving the girls an exercise room would only give them more reasons to fight. Some picked fights for no reason except to build drama.

On the short walk from the pod building to the gated corral, we walked in single file. My first thought was how easy it would be at this time to run away. A short-lived idea when I remembered the guns at the waist of the officers in front of us. Nonetheless, some of these girls can probably run fast, I wondered how often anyone has tried and what happened next. For me and my tiny stay, I planned on rolling through it with as good an attitude as possible. Some of the girls were serving years. I was shocked to learn that some of the girls were not even sentenced yet but were kind of being held. They just waited around in jail, how ghastly. They did not know what would become of themselves. No, I figured my life of crime was over here. Autonomy is highly favorable. I will be leaving in a month.

I talked to more girls when outside in the corral than I did inside the pod. This changed soon since I only got outside twice. A couple of girls opened up to me randomly and told me what had happened to them. Their husbands are trying to hold things together while they are incarcerated. They have troubles with parents or children. The girls spoke because they had to vent or commiserate but in all of my talks with them while I lived with them, I did not see any genuine repentance or plan for change. The blame for all ills landed on someone else. There were low personal responsibility skills among 90% of them. Older women were on the same page as me. They barely spoke, stayed as invisible as possible and prayed for time to pass. I thanked God every day for my cohesive family growing up, my family's rules, and my faith that sustained me. Witnessing so much hopelessness and depravity cramped into such a small space with no real program to teach or rehabilitate made me feel hopeless. What could be done for these girls? They were already so far gone from society.

The best part of going outside was watching the male police officers that were going to or from their cars in the parking lot across the road from our recreation hole. I have always been attracted to lawmen and I fantasized about these men now. If I wasn't wearing this orange jumpsuit, and my hair was combed, and blah- blah- blah. As long as I was in jail with these girls, it was as if I were one of them. That is the constant reaction I felt from all the other people I encountered. The guards discounted me like I was a criminal. I wanted to yell out, "I am not like them, this is an accident." Probably all the girls would say the same, but an observer could quickly determine that I was different from most of them.

The nurse came to the door to hand out meds before lunch call. She yelled out name after name, illegible. A girl came to my bunk and said that the nurse had called my name twice. I guess they were paying some attention to me if they knew my last name, which was as surprising as the nurse calling my name in the first place. This was unexpected since I had not yet spoken to anyone about my medicine besides the people that I felt sure were ignoring me. I sprang off the bunk and at the door was handed a tiny paper shot glass with one tablet inside. "Where's your water, where's your water?" She was losing her patience with me and I thought it was her fault. I stared at her blankly while she firmly told me to always fetch water in the coffee/chicory cup and bring it ready to the door when my name was called at med-time. It made sense of course, but I was just starting. How am I supposed to know the rules? No one explained anything. They (the officers) all assumed that each inmate was a repeat offender that was just living this lifestyle. People that were dropping in briefly had to block out this insult.

I had only received one half of my dosage but was grateful for it. I had taken my prescribed tablets for years faithfully and was nervous about playing around with changing my routine. I still did not know how much they would take from my account for the medicine because this was not the stuff that I had brought along. I learned later that the meds were free. I did not think this was prudent use of tax-payers money. This living for free was not a bad deal: free food, free medicine, free bunk and shower. What they say is true, some must remain criminals because it is sort of easier than having to actually support yourself, how nuts. These things cost decent people a lot of money and effort, crime seems to pay after all. Many times I wish they would provide sedatives to the obnoxious ones.

Lying on my bunk, I noticed the ceiling was like cottage cheese. Did my mind see everything in terms of food? I was impressed that the flouresant light cover was clean. Even in the cleanest homes, if there is dirt built-up, it will certainly be in this area. The cover must have been new; it sparkled compared to everything else around me. There was the ever-blasting cold air above me. I hoped that I could move to a new bunk soon, I dreamt of blessed wind-free sleep. Every doorway and window was labeled with a tiny number or a number plus a letter. This seemed like a military detail and the order made me feel comfortable. My father served in the Marines and he is perfect. Therefore, I like most things military. Discipline and structure are missing in so much of modern life that I am sure that is why these jail buildings are overcrowded.

The bookshelf choices kept recycling which was good, but rare were the pickings even so. The same romance novels sat there untouched. I found a thriller called *Sphere* that I read in a day. Marny made more points as one my favorites by pulling *Pilgrim's Progress* by Bunyan from her bin to loan me. This Christian classic was full of good imagery and I was delighted with it. I coveted it for my personal shelf at home. I stole it quickly to my bunk like a treasure. I read it in a day; God decided that day would be on May 17. Not many of the other girls read. I bonded with a woman close to my age and much prettier, her name was Carmen. She was calm and I felt kindred with her. After opening up with one another a bit we learned that each had been placed in jail because we let alcohol and fun take over our judgment at times (the only DUI convictions in the pod), that we were both close to God, and both traveled much throughout our lives. This was great news. I was like someone in there. She had a bin full of books and through her I read, *"Left Behind"* and *"Tribulation Force."*

The commissary order was due later this day and the girls were talking about nothing else. I wanted my t-shirt. I could have bought a long- sleeved thermal but I was too cheap. After all, I did not have parents, a husband or a boyfriend to add money each week. These girls were so wasteful and spoiled with other people's money. It was strange to witness this sense of entitlement. They forgot that the county was providing meals and basic hygiene items. How do we as a society fix this mess? I suppose the fracturing of the basic family unit is to blame. We must return to respecting the family and gaining a sense of personal responsibility. For a few seconds at a time on various days, I thought how fulfilling it could be to become a social worker. To make a difference in turning any one of these lives around would be quite something. Really, I more often felt the task would be harrowing. Patience is not my strongest trait and I now have more sympathy for any field of work that requires trying to bring the part of society that these girls have missed into their lives. I suppose that makes me a coward. It is impossible not to blame the parents.

The pod was called in sections into the cafeteria to check and pick up our orders when they arrived. It seemed a bit despicable that this commissary business played on and increased the irresponsibility of the girls. Making available (no matter that the cost was low) to the girls any manner of luxury items when they were supposed to be learning a lesson was nuts. The county made it easy and convenient for the girls to treat the jail as a regular home. There was no real incentive to change behaviors in the future. That sounded harsh but I tried and failed to see anything during my stay except the too few sessions in things like self-defeating behaviors and anger management. These girls needed constant immersion in the decent and acceptable (even high standard) behaviors of society. They did not seem to realize that most people do not live as they do and they did not care. Ending up in jail was just a process to get through (repeatedly). I will try not to go on a tangent about the state of society. God will have to fix that in His time, we are not doing a good job.

The first and second time I picked up my commissary order, I forgot to bring my pillow case from my bunk. Again, I did not know the routine, and the officers got angry at me. I lost my place in line and had to wait for my candy. How addicted am I to chocolate? I received my things, signed for them and hurried back to my bunk before anyone tried to hock my candy. The attendants were vigilant in claiming back the pen after an inmate signed. Pens in the pod would be contraband.

Some of the girls were shameless (well most- in one way or another);
they would take anything from you like we lived in socialism or
something. I made sure they knew that I had nothing left after I sucked
slowly on my chocolate. The pad of paper I got was a delight. The pencil
sharpener I finally found near the pay-phone was one of those crank-
types like in elementary school. It just went along with all the girls that
acted like they were still in grade school. The girls fought with people
on the other end of the phone endlessly. The screaming was usually
foundless. Petty things like the amount of money sent to docket
accounts or the way those left on the outside were handling the
inmate's affairs. I always thought, stop doing crime and you can stay out
of here and handle things yourself. I felt they would complain no matter
what.

Marny became my pod favorite, the beautiful girl of twenty-six.
Her bunk was on the bottom diagonally from mine. It took me a lot of
listening to gather information about the girl's situations. I suppose that
it was none of my business but curiosity got the best of me and besides I
had nothing but time on my hands. I might as well eavesdrop. Marny
had a young husband and a son on the outside. Her husband was many
years younger than her so I was proud of her in a cougar kind of way.
She wrote letters to him almost every day (the husband). I got the
impression that he was involved in crime and was out of jail at the
moment as a temporary reprieve. Marny was mad about him. She had
pictures that her son had drawn taped to the wall in her bunk. Every
time the officers would do a shakedown (more on that later) they
ripped them down from her area and all others. The girls should have
known that there precious memoirs would be ripped down but they still
continued to tempt the officers into seeming overly rude. It was just
one more example of the girls making trouble for themselves. Once I got
my pencil I had to fight off the temptation to doodle all over the wall by
my bunk. I didn't dare though; I planned to be a perfect inmate. I was
among the older inmates and felt a certain responsibility to show the

younger girls a decent example. It is unfortunate that this place has turned me into a judgmental monster.

I felt bad for Trish. She had to take responsibility for everybody's behavior. She tried to keep order and yelled a lot. I don't know where she got the patience. She often isolated on her bunk and simply coped by ignoring many girls approaching her with requests all the time. She tried to keep the order for appearances sake by yelling but she knew as well as the rest that her efforts were in vain. She was a mystery to me at first. I wondered why she had this responsibility. I learned later that loud Lateasha had been the previous pod monitor. This was hard to believe since she was the worst behaved of everyone, how could she be in charge? It came at a time about a week into my stay that a petition was going around in the room via a form 62 that intended to oust Lateasha from the pod. I did not sign it because I did not want to get on anyone's bad side. I would just mind my own business and deal with any irritations as temporary. Another example of my cowardice or wisdom, I am not sure which.

She was gone before I noticed. There was still plenty of noise at night to not have missed her all that much. Now that her bunk was empty, the whole room wanted to claim it and this caused a domino effect. Ricky and I moved across the aisle. I was still on top and there was now no air vent over my bunk. What a blessing. Also, at night, smoke from officers or other workers outside the vented window did not waft in and choke me now. I often tried to see people out there smoking. Strangely, I never saw them but I smelled the effects. It must have been hard for the girls that were smokers to get a whiff of their coveted smoke and they were denied the privilege. I hoped that since these girls had gone so long without a cigarette that they may be able to refrain once they get back out there. It is probably an optimistic idea since all they seem to talk about is getting back to their old ways.

Some of the crimes that the people in my pod were charged/convicted of were DUI (me), battery, attempted murder (very comforting), prostitution, trafficking, writing bad checks, counterfeiting, shop-lifting, and parole/probation violations. Many of the girls used aliases while in jail. I found this out when I heard them talking about their real names. It fired many of the girls up with threats.

Now that the commissary had arrived, trades and begging began in force. Begging was a real problem in the pod. I had culture shock. I also held no sympathy for these mal-adjusts. I have never been able to comprehend this mindset. I know the girls are fed, the county feeds them well. They still have the nerve to expect (and I mean expect) the others to give them commissary food. Many fights started this way. I shook my head and was glad I had nothing for them to desire. I started getting nervous about my pencil going missing. I hid it as well as I could. I was writing continuously. My pencil was soon too small to hold without cramping my hand. Commissary sheets were available every Sunday and Thursday. I kept close track because when Trish announced that the forms had arrived, you had to act quickly to obtain one. Once the supply she was given was exhausted, Trish could get more but she was unreliable about it. I was going to order a new pencil and a pair of knee socks this time. My feet were always cold even though I often kept my sneakers on in bed. This was against the rules but Brrr. Now that I had moved into the bunk on the other side of the room, Linda suddenly started talking to me. She kept telling me how happy she was because I was so quiet. Quiet was indeed in short supply.

I liked the new bunk better anyway. Now I could sit up and face the main area instead of sitting up and staring at the bathroom traffic. I learned that Linda was married to a much older man. She called him her old man; I had not heard this expression in many years. She was kind of old herself. She was with him because he tolerated her crimes and paid the bills for the both of them. She was into heavy drugs. Like the others, she said that getting the drug she wanted would be her first stop on the way out of jail. She also hated her daughter because she (the daughter) had seduced Linda's husband and he now paid for her bills as well. What a dysfunctional mess. Linda had a bad back so she had a funny way of making her bed. She doubled up her mattress and this left the bottom half of her body lying on the metal. She said she had asked for but was denied a second mattress. She was very quiet and became one of my favorite pod-mates. If she was agitated she paced, made faces, and mumbled to herself. I think she was afraid to really confront the younger ones because they could easily hurt her.

It was good for me that I was allowed to get outside again the next day. No one seemed mad about it. After lapping with a girl that told me about how her and her husband's business was going to hell now that she was in here, I sat in the sun by the fence. This was a good place to stretch. Many of the lappers nearly stepped on me as I lay back on the paved area. I was philosophical about being inside the fence when the officers were outside the fence laughing and living. I felt I had befallen a tragedy but in the happiest possible way. Nothing was going on in my life while I took a break from it. It was short term compared to most of my new (friends)? I started to wonder what in the world God could possibly have planned to lead this into something good.

There was another girl named Marny and I really liked her at first. She seemed normal enough. She loaned me a book to read and I suddenly bonded with her because of that. After more observation over the next days, I found myself rejoicing when her release day came. She was older and put her hair in different styles several times a day. At night when they would all tune into the same radio station, she danced shamelessly with the younger girls. They all looked like strippers but I guess the younger ones just look better at it (of course), crazy Marny looked pathetic. She would have crying bouts at random. She may have been genuinely nuts. Often she would walk through the pod talking to someone that was not there loudly and violently flailing her arms about. One day a girl was going to throw away a really neat pair of socks. The striped knee-high kind. I said. "Socks, can I have them." My feet were crying from the cold.

I claimed them and hid them but soon I saw Marny wearing them. Some of the other girls wanted to fight her on my behalf since she had stolen them from my bunk. I thought it wasn't worth it, but was secretly affronted. She was one of the first to get released while I was part of the pod. The girls talked of nothing else in the days leading up to their big day.

When the day came, the officer came in after breakfast when the lights had been dimmed again. They yelled the lucky departer's name from the door. Other times they called on the intercom and the girl had better be ready at the door with her things together by the time the escort made it to the pod door. It was Salet (always the last name), roll it up (grab your mattress and your things), you are being released. So the girls knew they would get out about 5:00am. After breakfast they might camp by the door. This worked unless a crabby officer was on guard. In that case it was back to the bunk to wait there.

I did not know that the pod was in lock down each day directly after lunch. Another thing that I was supposed to know without being told. Lock down meant that each girl was to remain in their own bunk and be still until the officers said it was alright. I think this was to give the assigned cleaning teams a chance to sweep and mop without bodies everywhere. As expected, some of the girls in each cleaning team slacked off and watched the others do the work. Certain girls would take the time to move the bins and shoes to mop under the bunks. Others just ran the mop through the middle. The meticulous girls left us much cleaner and organized but the slackers got us off of lock down faster. I never cared much about lockdown; I rarely had plans to leave my bunk anyway. I was horrified early on when I was showering right after lunch (a no-no). I did not have to endure the wrath of the officers because some observant girls came and forced me out of the shower before I was found out. Lockdown was a joke. The girls talked about how much they hated it but their behavior barely changed whether we were under lockdown or not. The TV was kept off but the girls surely did not stay in their bunks.

Lockdown meant nothing except more imaginary things for the girls to complain about. The no TV was a huge problem for the complaining girls. I bet most of the inmates in my pod have never opened a book. I read nine books while I was there, and that small number is due to the lack of available books and my writing notes all the time.

Something exciting happened after about a week. I was in the right place at the right time because when an officer came in to the pod and asked if anyone wanted a haircut, I made myself known before the other girls even heard what she had offered. Soon, everyone wanted a trim. I was first and was ushered to the cafeteria where a makeshift salon had been created. The hair-dresser was another inmate from one of the other pods. I never understood the dynamics of this haircutting process. The service was offered in the jail handbook. I know because since it had words, I read it front to back. I got my new style and returned to brag inwardly to the others. I learned soon that the girls that cut the hair expected tips for the service. Where was I supposed to get money? When I asked someone, the answer was that you buy them what they want from commissary. I did not go for this. I stuck with my conservation plan.

I rarely washed my hair. It was too cold. Some of the younger girls were washing their hair every day. Not to mention the waste of shampoo, the idea was too painful to consider often. I stuck to suffering only once a week. What's the difference? I was not trying to attract anyone. Even at home, twice a week holds me. I did not have a comb for about two weeks anyway. When I did wash my hair, it just remained a mangled mess. When I spent the few cents on the comb it was not much better. Without any conditioner, it was close to impossible to comb through my hair. Not only would I be even colder with a wet head but we were only allowed one towel each. The towel would not dry well after the soaking of a wet head. This meant that during the next shower, the towel would still be wet from the day before. It was better to have dirty hair. There was no great place to hang a towel to dry and there were forty of us. Sometimes I would have to just lay the towel flat across my blanket to dry. This made my bunk damp and it was never as warm as I would have liked.

I let the hair on my legs grow gnarly for the added warmth. It worked out well since it was hard to shave your legs in the shower. One leg had to get lifted and braced on the wall which meant leaning your butt and lower back onto the tiles for balance. What else could a girl do? I was not about to sit on the shower floor like I do in some hotels when left with only a standing unit. I hope that I could trust the cleanliness of a hotel room I had paid good money for. Who knew what these chicks did in the shower. The water was always hot though, a blessing.

Whip was created by using drink mix of any flavor and water vigorously whipped with a fork. The fork was not allowed in the pod, but girls snuck them into the waistbands of their fashion slacks from meals. I admit, that I ordered hot chocolate and single serve coffee packets from the commissary toward the end of my stay (I guess I longed for variety after all) and brought spoons back from the cafeteria a few times. This whip was handed around to a group of girls to take turns giving their best effort at hard whipping. It was the most popular thing to do on commissary day and the girls ate it all fast and then complained that it was gone. I believe they craved it so much because it acted like a drug to them since it was all they could get. The sugar was getting them high. They tested it over and over to decide if the consistency was right. If not, more wrist action.

As far as I saw, they all shared this willingly with each other. It was a real group activity. I watched most of the time but tasted it twice. It was gross really, but I instantly knew the reason they loved it. It gave the classic sugar high. This was not at all what these girls needed. They used the bowls that came with the rice dishes or cereal they bought from commissary. The hot water in the bathroom offered the only chance to make coffee, soup, noodles, or whatever else. It worked well enough. I learned after about a week that this whip was forbidden. The officers did not want a room full of forty girls hopped up on pure sugar. Whenever there was a shakedown, the bowls and forks would be taken out of the room.

Shakedowns were for intimidation and genuine concern for everyone's best interest (safety wise). It was easy to get angry at the way the officers conducted these invasions until I remembered that I was on their side. I forced myself to look at things from the law enforcement's perspective. Most often a group of police would come into the pod randomly and begin overturning mattresses, going through pillowcases, examining the contents of the under-bunk bins, and all around leaving a nice mess behind. As I mentioned about the intimidation factor, this exhibition clearly showed the girls who was in charge and they hated it. All table wear that had been stolen from the cafeteria was taken. If a bin had any extra toothpaste-razors-shampoo (county issue) they were taken. I learned that trying to stockpile maxi pads from the bathroom under my mattress was stupid, they took those too.

Each night when the inmate cleaning lady would service our bathroom, she left maxi pads laying everywhere. I did not want to be low when I needed them so I snuck them to my bunk whenever I could. It was getting lumpy under my mattress. I now had my shoes, books, my writing pad, and maxi pads under there. Certain days were set aside for receiving a fresh set of clothes, another for a fresh towel and sheets, and still another for toothpaste-razor-shampoo. These basics were fine for me. When the call came from the door for toothpaste or razor switch, we were expected to take our used one and exchange them for fresh. Shampoo was different, we brought out small bottles to the door and the officer pumped shampoo into the same bottles. I used my shampoo for body soap most of the time so I never missed a shampoo call. Come to think of it, the liquid was probably meant to be soap and I was just using it as shampoo also. I still did not know what was really going on. Most of the girls wasted their commissary money on fancy products though, very strange for jail I thought. One of the things that creeped me out the most about my time in the county jail was that since forty girls shared the pod; probably at least ten of them had their period at any given time. Try not to imagine the condition of the toilet area. It was shocking to me the way people behave. When looking over my notes, I found a sentence that wrapped up my disgust. I wrote, *"Some are real slobs, no flush, leave blood on toilet, wrap nozzle with maxi pad."*

People started telling me that I would only have to serve twenty days of my thirty day sentence. This meant I should be on my best behavior. I often heard the officers threaten the girls with longer stays if they did not stop fighting, stealing, or having temper tantrums. This news excited me and as it turned out the initial time during my arrest counted as two days, so I had to only stay eighteen days. I hoped this was true but did not trust my sources completely. I wrote a 62 which said, "I believe my release date is on June 2nd. Is this true?" It was ignored. My peace of mind was not on the officer's priority list. I did, however; suddenly draw a calendar into my note pad and X out the days as they passed.

The laundry bag was hung under the TV. I paid no attention to it since no one told me the protocol. Anyway, I was flipping my undies and using maxi pads as panty liners to keep my undies in usable condition. It was Trish that had to pass out the laundry when it was brought in clean. She went above the call of duty by folding everything. Some girls had a lot of shirts, ect. The first laundry day that I paid attention to, Marny had her long sleeve thermal go missing. She wanted to fight with everyone accusing them of thievery. It would be simple to just take anything out of the hanging laundry bag before the inmate laundry workers took it out. I think it was once a week, but I am not sure- only sent out my socks and t-shirt once. Sure enough, my t-shirt did not come back to me. I felt just like Marny had. I did not start any fight about it, but made subdued but obvious verbal complaints into thin air. I needed my t-shirt; I thought I may freeze to death in there.

My t-shirt showed up the next day. That was peculiar, where had it been? It had been in someone's bin or on their body that's where. All of the clothes bought from commissary had to be labeled with a Sharpie-marker. The markers were forbidden, so we had to use a form 62 each time we had to use one.

My name was called one day shortly before dinner. Dinner was about 4:30pm. It was the early bird special of the day after day after day. Not knowing what I was summoned about, I only feared I would miss my meal. The escort only walked me to another room in the building so I could explain my medicine need to a nurse. The medicine situation was very haphazard. I was questioned formally after I had been receiving aspirin for over a week. I explained my medical history and they gave me a form to fill out. This form wanted details about my doctor's information and so forth. Certainly no information I had handy under my mattress. I wrote my former doctor's name, the city, and that was all. It had been years since my stroke. I was just doing what he prescribed at the time. Six-hundred and fifty milligrams of aspirin a day for the rest of my life to keep my blood thin. I returned the form and still only got one tablet per day in the morning instead of the two that I needed. No one cared that I had thought ahead and brought all of the paperwork about the need with me but that it was somewhere locked up in a baggy in the abyss called property.

On May 22, I awoke happy. Napping after breakfast, I awoke to the call to meds. The rounds could not be predicted. The cart was supposed to come around once in the morning and once at night. There are times when the girls waited until nearly bedtime to get their night meds. Sometimes the meds cart would interfere with the call to meals.

It was strange how they could not get the meds on a more regular schedule; God knows that the meals were.

Arnold yelled my name from the door and I sprang from my bunk. Whenever my name was called, I sprang from the bunk as to not keep the officer of the moment waiting. They got very mad if you did not come to the door immediately. I felt bad for those that were in the showers at this time. I had my water cup in hand and waited in line behind the others. My turn came and I peered into the tiny cup and did not recognize the tablet. Fear gripped my chest. I protested that I did not want to take the pill since I did not know what it was. It surely was not what I had been taking. It was not aspirin. Arnold told me that it was the correct tablet. Were they doing an experiment on me or drugging me into submission? I was already the most submissive one in the pod.

Arnold was a large, blonde woman with a gruff manner although by the end of my stay, she had become one of my favorite officers. I reluctantly swallowed the pill. I was nervous. I went back to my bunk and wrote a form 62. I nearly wrote a book on the tiny form. At this point, I thought I was going to get charged for any medicine that they gave me. I did not have any extra money, I did not want to eat mystery medicine, and my brain wanted aspirin. I could not get any peace about what to do; I did not want to cause trouble. I vowed to refuse the pill the next day if it was not right. The 62 stayed under my mattress for a day before I put my trust in the Lord and ripped it up.

The two days of outside recreation I enjoyed during the first week was all the daylight I was to get. After the last time, it stormed and the yard became too muddy. The officers would not let us out. This was very bad for morale. Pretty soon, Julia was pacing the room constantly. Fights broke out often between her and others. She was quick and her buzzing around made me think she might be crazy. While she burned off her food by running people over in the aisle, others were gaining weight. So much extra commissary food was consumed out of boredom that girls started comparing their stomach rolls.

Even though I only had two candy bars on commissary days. I was getting fat too. I wrote in my notes that I was consuming forty-two pieces of bread a week. Probably more since I sometimes traded things for it. Also, lots of rice and pasta were served. One of my favorite dishes was also the most simple. Curly noodles were served with shavings of celery and carrots. There was no sauce on it. Ice cold and starchy, I could have eaten it at every meal.

A disturbing thing happened to me in the cafeteria on my sixth day. A girl I had not seen before sat a few tables away facing my direction. She was gorgeous. She had short reddish hair. I swear, she looked like a fabulous young boy. I could not keep my eyes off of her. What was this about? I had trouble convincing myself that it was a girl. My attraction to her unsettled me. She was just so gorgeous in a well-groomed young man kind of way. I was relieved to never see her again. Verbatim from my notes-6th day dinner, shocked and distracted- in mess hall- a girl (shaved head), very young- looked like a gorgeous boy- shame on me- I couldn't keep my eyes off her. I think I would have trouble sentencing someone so young and pretty- she was a gorgeous boy.

Chapter Eight

On the day that we changed out our clothes, an officer came around with large carts. The inmates traded the dirty for the clean at the door. Since everyone had only one set, this meant stripping down to undies and dressing temporarily in the bunk linen. Not all of the girls wore the same color suits. Most were orange like mine, but there was also green and blue. The girls that wore blue were called blueberries. I wished I was a blueberry even though I have no idea what the difference was. I only knew that blue was a calm color and it was a nice shade. The orange was obnoxious and the green was boring. I did learn that the girls dressed in green were felons or charged with a felony. At first I thought someone said that the felonies and misdemeanors were separated, lack of space must have forced us together. After the first week, I asked for a larger pair of pants. I was eating carbohydrates like mad and barely moving from my bunk. It was similar to being a cat or an infant, just eating and sleeping.

An embarrassing thing happened to me regarding my orange pants at a certain time of the month. Tampons were unavailable so maxi-pads had to be worn during my period. I never trust them because whenever I sleep, accidents happen. I thought ahead and put two on so they overlapped. Well, bloody hell (no pun intended), just a short nap and I leaked all over my pants. I do not understand how even the best preparation in these matters is futile. It is true that tampons are less healthy than the alternative but I will take my chances to avoid the maxi-pad enigma. These had wings too but still the issue got out. I hate these stupid wings. Without fail, I secure the wings to my undies and as soon as I pull up my pants, I realize that the placement is wrong. It's a project every change.

I took off my pants and wrapped my blanket around my butt. At the glass partition window, I waved frantically to gain an officer's attention. I had never singled myself out like this before and it made me nervous as well as embarrassed. She opened the door and said, "What is it?" I plainly said that I had bled all over my pants; can I get a fresh pair? After telling her the size, she delivered them instantly. If anyone noticed me acting strangely no one said a word. I was either well liked and the girls had sympathy for me not to heckle me or I was truly invisible in the room.

They kept busy playing games at the tables while others watched the TV. Some of the games on the shelves included Sorry, Monopoly, Backgammon, and they had playing cards. One thing I would have liked available is coloring books and crayons. I have always entertained myself with this child's distraction throughout my adulthood.

I never joined them while they played but sometimes I sat at the tables with them reading. The girls fought constantly about everything when they related to one another. It was a bit humorous, scary, and unbelievable at alternating times. My body ached from the lack of exercise and using any excuse to leave the bunk was my time to stretch. There were plastic chairs at the end of each bunk bed aisle. Once in a while I would sit in one and read for a change of scenery around the room but I always felt the girls resented me for it. I am not sure why. I think partially because some of the girls in the upper bunks used these chairs as personal step-stools up onto their bunks. I received many dirty looks. Plastic bags filled with toilet paper hung on the bunk posts in the aisles.

After lights out, the chairs filled with girls that had to sit there nearer the glare from the bathroom lights if they wanted to read. When they heard a click of the door handle they ran back to their bunks. The readers and the late night singers and dancers tripped all over each other. Sue returned late from her "job" every night. I do not know what she did, but she was important to the others. She distributed messages between pods, brought in extra food from the cafeteria, and told jokes. Since she was very large, watching her tell jokes and laugh was fun. She was like a black female Santa Claus. She was very sweet and had children waiting outside. It seems like there may have been hope for her. She did not seem hell-bent on getting into immediate trouble again and talked about her babies a lot. I never asked anyone but wondered what trouble she could make. She must have been arrested as an accomplice to someone else's crime. She was just so jolly, sweet, innocent, and likeable.

A card game that certain girls played often was tarot cards. It upset me greatly. God does not abide this kind of thing and therefore neither do I. My main proof of this comes from studying the scripture books of Samuel. Marny (old, crazy) was the main tarot reader. She read the fortunes (??) of the girls one after the other, sometimes the same girl many times in a row. I always thought that a reader needed certain cards to really read tarot cards, but Marny and others were using regular playing cards. Who taught them how to do this? It scared me a little. Now I felt hopeless for the girls. It seemed to me when they joined in the tarot cards that they were not only girls being bad but girls being evil. Once Marny got released, I do not remember the tarot card cycle happening anymore.

Happy day. The air-conditioner broke. I even took my socks off and wiggled my freed toes. It was pleasant in the pod for the first time. I rushed to wash my hair. The girls were happy for about three hours and then complained so bitterly you'd think the officers had a personal hand in breaking the air-handler to vex the girls. I am sure the officers did much to vex the girls for intimidation sake, but this was likely not one of those times. The same girls that did not like the cold cried just as hard at the warmth, classic. The smell would have gotten funky had the problem (what problem) persisted for too long. The entire episode lasted less than one day. I would have taken the odor over the painful cold, either way I did not say a word.

A more important and real problem happened in the pod less than a week after the air broke. The plumbing started to back up. This was a true mess. Now we really did have an odor problem and my bunk was in the section closest to the source. The toilet at the left would pour water from its base into the center of the room at each flush. When any of the toilets were flushed, black debris laden water would bubble up from the floor drain flooding the toilet area, and one of the showers suddenly would not drain. As gross as it sounds, many were trying to convince the others to stop flushing the toilets. It is hard to imagine the result with forty or more girls in the pod at any given time. The black ooze flooding was rank and when it would settle back down into the floor, it had to be mopped endlessly. A few brave girls kept up with this. Plumbers came into the pod two days in a row and finally the problem faded away. It was clear that this pod may be ready for retirement. It is hard on the county, however; since the criminals do not seem ready to retire, they just keep coming.

I moved bunks again. The top bunk diagonal from me became available. I guess I craved a change of scenery because I asked Trish first and had my mattress thrown up onto the new bunk before any others could protest. I did enjoy getting a new perspective again but I immediately found a fault in my new home. There was another air vent above this bed. I had been hasty just for a change and forgot my sweet wind-free sleep. I did something daring. I felt like the criminal I was. The officers would have made an example out of me if they found out what I did. Thank God that no one even noticed. I kept the trick to myself also in case someone had something against me and wanted to rat me out. I ripped a few pages from my notepad and forced them up under the edge of the vent grate. This worked beautifully. I know the officers were very observant and I over-worried about the lecture I would receive if found out. The white paper blended in decently with the paint. I got away with it. This new bunk had better dismounting steps. I no longer had to fear the wrath of anyone below me. The steps hurt my feet if only socked. I blamed the trouble getting in and out of the bunk on my age. I was getting stiffer and stiffer with all the inactivity.

It was about this time that Mercedes (now below me) reminded me of what I had said on my first day when the girls helped me tie my sheets. She said I was funny that day when I said, "I'm just starting." I did not remember saying that but now thought it might be a nice title for the memoirs of this love/hate life situation. I found this exchange on page thirteen of my notes. Linda also commented that since I was always writing that I would make a good journalist. I have no real call to be a journalist but thought more seriously about my notes after that. Mercedes talked to me more often after I moved to the bunk above her. She showed me a photo of her lingerie-clad girlfriend. She gave me spoonfuls of instant coffee, and let me use her good shampoo. Out of all the girls, Mercedes and I hit it off the best. I thought it was strange that she had a girlfriend since she was in jail for a prostitution charge. She was adorable and made me laugh no matter what she was guilty of.

I ran into Mercedes at a convenient store about a year after my release. We hugged but parted ways quickly. She seemed involved with some folks that I meant to get away from, so I hope she has stayed out of trouble.

My attendance for the AA meeting that I signed up for was delayed but I heard my name called from the door for the seven o'clock meeting in my second week. The meeting was held in the cafeteria. Sadly, the thing I remember the most about this meeting was talking to a woman about her silver ring. I had to turn over all my jewelry into property and I felt a little jealous. The feeling was similar to the pang I felt when I saw others wearing their regular shoes. I wanted my Roswell shoes and now I wanted my silver band back on my finger also.

Actually, I got more from the meeting than just envy. I was brand new to AA at this time and was interested in what the other girls thought about it. I had received a big blue book from a form 62 order that I put in to request one. I had already finished a super large print copy. I wanted another one anyway to keep under my own mattress. The chairperson was allowed into the jail once a week to lead an AA meeting. She was doing a great service and I was shocked when she told me how her attempts to get in more often had been blocked. This made me feel early on in my stay that the county really did not want to do much to help these girls get better. True, they were in jail for punishment but I thought simple things that did not cost the county anything could be a great benefit to the girls. They needed exposure to alternative lifestyles than what they had and planned to return to as soon as possible. An available meeting each night would make more sense. On second thought, maybe they did not want the girls from the different pods to have the chance to mingle too regularly. There may be some red-tape or political reason why AA was only allowed in once a week but I thought it was a real shame. I felt the same way about the self-defeating behavior class. The instructor was a social worker and she related well to everyone. She really got the girls involved through writing assignments and direct questions. It was too bad that so many of the girls only attended to see their friends in other pods.

The turnout was good. Fifteen or twenty girls made a circle around the table. The chairwoman started by showing some pictures of her grandchildren. After that it was like any other meeting. Few girls wanted to share their feelings but listening to others is as important. The funny thing to me was if the girls had been in jail and obviously were not drinking, why they needed support to quit. They already had. When I thought this I was new to the program's ideals and now realize that the support needs to be permanent for someone that really has an addiction to the drink. I talked for a minute to point out the acceptance chapter of the big blue book. I will transcribe the brief section here as the sentences can benefit anyone. Alcoholics Anonymous Big Book Edition Four- page 417:

Acceptance is the answer to all my problems today. When I am disturbed it is because I find some person, place, thing, or situation- some fact of my life- unacceptable to me, and I find no serenity until I accept that person, place, thing, or situation as being exactly the way it is supposed to be at this moment. Nothing, absolutely nothing happens in God's world by mistake.

It was my favorite part of the big book. As a Christian, I have faith that my days and minutes are directed by the Lord and I can't do a thing about it. One of my favorite Scripture verses reads, "Man's goings are of the Lord, how than can a man understand his own way?"

The meeting went well, and even after trying to be spiritual, I still wanted my ring on my finger. The reason the other woman was allowed to keep hers was because she could not get it off of her hand. For such a military style place, I noticed many exceptions made to the rules. I was happy to return to my bunk afterwards. I had been reading my new recovery Bible a lot. Texts I had studied and loved my whole life comforted me. I was fortunate to have always attended Bible churches and my knowledge of Scripture was very good. I loved it. For years I had been estranged from my commitment to Christ, the time in county jail allowed me to reacquaint myself with my first love.

I was starting to feel more comfortable in the room. Not that I hoped to extend my stay but I no longer felt worried about how the girls reacted to me. Most liked my private-ness. I merely observed about 90% of the time.

I'm Just Starting 100

Chapter Nine

The officers that guarded us and cared for us grew on me for the most part. I am tempted to sketch caricatures of them in the margins here. It will suffice for me to describe them later (see Appendix B). That would jeopardize the anonymity of giving my stars aliases. During my stay, I came to like each of them despite their harshness toward us. They had hard jobs and deserved respect. I caught them acting human quite often. It was funny watching them get confused when coming into the pods at night. The girls switched bunks so often, the officers would look for a certain girl and we were all silent while she searched the many faces until she found her charge. They always found a reason to yell at the room at large so we knew who was going home that night and who was staying. This brings to memory a shakedown that brought a double duty of officers into the pod. We each had to pull our bins out and stand near our bunks but out of the way. We had shakedowns before but this time Mercedes handed me a hair tie and told me to put my hair up. I looked at Ricky with questioning eyes. She said, "Just do it."

A handsome officer that I had not seen before joined the search through the room. I kept moving between girls so that wherever this man walked, I could get a look at him. What a relief that I am still attracted to men. Of course, I felt a little like a fool; an inmate that looked like a sloppy wreck making eyes at an officer while he looked for contraband was pathetic. Even a well-groomed attractive inmate doing the same still would be pathetic. I think about the reference in Dante's *Inferno* when the lost souls spoke of the heavenly angels walking through the layers of hell with no regard for the residents of the bleak mire. The officers viewed us the same way, lost, hopeless, and bad. The search seemed especially vigorous as if they had a real suspicion instead of just an intimidation agenda.

The usual things were taken and I learned that the hair tie was because there had been a lice scare in the pod. After the officers left and the mattresses were replaced onto the bunks, Mercedes rubbed some goo into my hair. She said it was for protection from lice. I let her apply it but my hair was already pretty dirty, it felt gross. More people started wearing braids all of a sudden. The salon was always open- 24/7. The braiding sometimes took more than an hour to complete. It was a hobby for a lot of them. No different than my reading and writing I suppose.

At the entrance to the bathroom on the right was a door to the outside with a glass window rectangle. I liked to stand there and stare outside. I would pray and look up at the sky. Sometimes I watched cars pull in and out of the driveways that were in view and wonder about the driver's lives. I spent a lot of time there and so did Julia. At times, a chair would be there waiting for a reader searching for some natural light. What I could have done without is that this is also where the girls that liked each other would make out. The bunks toward the front of the room near the windows by the officers were reserved for certain girls. It seems that if you were caught fooling around with another girl in a bunk, you were moved to the front for closer surveillance. The lesbian thing became a philosophical conundrum in my mind. What the public hears rumored about jail was true in the observations I made. Without exaggeration, most of the girls in my pod had girlfriends and they often went about holding hands and kissing. More power to them if that is their thing. I just wondered how it could be nearly universal among the girls. Were they pretending so that they would fit in? My unanswered question remains. Does spending a lot of time in jail turn a girl into a lesbian or is a lesbian more apt to end up in jail because of societal recrimination? I don't know and I surely would feel too awkward interviewing criminals or lesbians to get an answer.

Marty, the girl that did not like my swingy legs at my first bunk had a girlfriend. The second girl was Cora. I am uninitiated in the lesbian world; I could not tell which was playing the male role and which was playing the female role. I do know that they fought like a married couple. Cora was quiet but had a deep voice. I liked having her in my area because she was respectful of the others. I had to forgive her when she had to yell to protect herself from the highly sensitive Marty.

I had dreams every night about different men that were my friends on the outside. It seems subconsciously, I missed having men around me. I have rarely been one to hang around with women. This super submersion was getting old. I got to hang out with Bob, Steve, Chris, Zoltan, and Ron in my sleep. I knew that I would have to wean myself from hanging around with Bob, Chris, and Zoltan on the outside if I was to continue in sobriety. I have succeeded. We are all still friends but in a much more talk to you on the phone once in a while kind of a way.

Sadly, I had one day of reflection into my past. Steve and I had a long and unseemly relationship which ended but which I have never recovered from properly. That is where the haunting comes from. It seems about once a year if I allow myself to reminisce, that I have a crying fit that resembles a break down. This will be one of the first things I ask God to explain to me when I get to heaven. Steve often pops into my dreams and mostly I can shake it off, mostly- but not every time.

Before I woke up I had been sitting on a swing, one of the types in a school playground. Steve was sitting on a bleacher bench not far from where I pushed myself slowly forward and backwards with my foot. He watched kids playing softball on the field and he was eating a piece of pizza. I wanted the pizza. Steve did not look my way but I was intent on him. A friend of mine came by where I sat swinging to dump sand from his shoes. Steve was very interested in the game and I tried to get rid of my friend so that I could peacefully stare at Steve with wonder. Quickly Steve approached me and hugged and kissed me. We both turned to look at my friend who was now watching the game intently.

It was ridiculous, I sobbed into my pillow for twenty minutes hoping to remain anonymous. No one noticed my grief. I have always felt stupid about this because it is self-induced. The dreamy intimacy between my love and myself left me sad because it was only going to be possible in a dream. I should have learned how to control this in my self-defeating behavior class. The non-closure has stalked me for over ten years. I forced my way from the memories and pulled the blankets down away from my head. Back in the room, I observed that no one had missed me while I isolated. A good thing about jail is that despite the fact that (in my case) dozens of other people are within a few feet of you, it is easy to be alone.

To block out some of the noise, I learned how to made earplugs out of flip-flops. For over a week I thought something was peculiar about so many black and white flops strewn all over the place with a set of perfect holes in them. If I had observed the girls creating their own noise reducers, my mind overlooked it. It was not until I asked Mercedes what the mystery was that she pulled out a tiny county issued toothpaste tube. Forcing the cap's outer rim into the rubber of the footwear and twisting and twisting produced the perfect ear-sized cut-outs. Brilliant. I felt proud when I was able to later teach this trick to Melody, a newcomer in a green outfit that had joined our section. Making the earplugs was forbidden but the officers just blithely told the room to stop it. I kept my shoes and ear plugs hidden on the metal rim of my bed closest to the wall.

When Melody arrived she looked scared to death. I soon sympathized with her because she did not look like a criminal like the others. What I mean by that is that she was not covered with tattoos nor did she have a hard obstinate countenance. I do not mean to deride tattoo wearers; I have been a fan of them on men my whole life, often approaching strangers to ask them to lift their sleeves to reveal the complete art. The request always followed by, "What else have you got," or "You are getting more right." The problem with the girls in my pod was that unbelievably most had tattoos displayed on their necks. This was a shock to my conservative constitution at first. I did and still think that tattoos on women are unacceptable. It represents a double standard perhaps but I am no feminist.

The new generation seemed oblivious to the future and seemed to deny their place in it. Without wearing a scarf every day, these girls will never hold a reputable career position. It is true that society is changing its attitude about certain customs. I think this is a mistake. By lowering the standard of society by small degrees, the combined result will leave society with no ethics to stand on. Instead of tolerating anti-social behavior more we should stress raising the bar and creating more excellent people. No one wants to read *Jan loves Lisa* on a girl's neck while ordering fast food, even less so in a board room. I am grateful for the times my mom told me I looked like a hussy. She let me know what I wore for my presentation to the world was unacceptable. Of course, I thought she was harsh and out of touch, but she proved correct. Maybe a lot of the girls in jail with me never had a mother that cared to teach them to respect themselves and society at large. This sad reality left me sick to my stomach because it was too late for mothering at this point for them.

Melody was charged with battery by her parents. Since she was older than me, her folks must have been in their seventies. I did not want to believe that this blonde woman that could have been me was capable of force against senior citizens. That seemed cowardly and I hoped she told the truth when she denied the charge. The more she talked to me over the next few days though; I started to see a bad pattern. She told me that she held a master's degree and that she was a teacher. I wondered why she said she did not have a penny to her name or even a home. Where is my commiserative compassion?

I never found out but suspect that either drugs or alcohol had something to do with the problem. Given the atmosphere I lived in lately, trust is fragile at best. I prayed that the problem with her parents, her husband, and her finances could be reconciled and they would all find peace in their interconnectedness. She was gone like a vapor one day when I returned from the shower room.

I wondered how whip might taste if it was made with a hot chocolate packet. The wait between commissary days and my two candy bars left me craving. I did not want to join the girls in whip mania nor did I want to give the officers any reason to call me out. It was bad enough I was treading closely to rebellion with my wind blocking paper rig. As I read over my note pages from my stay, I laughed at how many times I wrote about the candy bars. They had become my anticipated life source, chocolate was really like a drug. I had to concentrate hard on the Scripture where it says, "Make no provision for the flesh." With the meals we sometimes received a dessert of sorts.

It looked like a square of cake. I am not sure what it was though, it was very dry. It was simply county jail cake. It did not fill the need but the peanut butter and honey in the morning did. If someone wanted to part with their serving, I held my hand out every time. I was quick to give away my wilted oranges, but everything else, I ate with happiness.

In order to receive a visitor, pre-arrangement had to be scheduled. A list would be posted on the glass window about who had slots of time allotted during that day. I was surprised at the method. It seemed like a lot of orchestration and logistics to get a visitor. Some of my friends said they would drop by to visit me. This endearing gesture would not have done anything except cause them to waste the gas in their cars to make the drive up there to see me. I bet this happened a lot to unsuspecting visitors.

For our mini unit, there was a tiny room with three TVs in a rigged communication room. The husband, mother, or whoever was visiting got broadcasted in from some other location in the complex. The inmate could only communicate with them by phone as they saw their image on the screen. There would be no privacy as the other two girls that also had visitors sat feet away on either side. This hardly seemed like a visit at all. The girls were left in the locked room alone with the other girls and the TVs but I bet that there was also another TV monitoring device in the officer's haven in the front of the building. It is a shame that the state of society and the human condition makes it so that suspicion has to be the name of the game. Then again these were criminals. Rarely did I notice a woman/girl return from a visit without drama following. The girls did have a proclivity toward violence. A disgruntled girl might decide to break the TV set over another girl's head. Since I only glanced inside the room and did not enter myself, I really do not know how the TVs were set up. Maybe they were just flattened into the wall. A well placed fist may have broken the screen.

Expectations of the inmate with the realities of what was happening in their lives in their absence clashed sometimes violently. People returned to the pod room swearing, ready to fight and destroy things. Instead of deciding to make a change in their lives they unanimously wanted to get out and get some type of revenge. They did not understand that the people in their lives were living without them. As often as not the scheduled visitor did not show up. This is when I saw the girls cry. They were so needy. Again I felt self-righteous. I lived alone and spent my time at home reading and writing. I told my friends and co-workers to think of me but not to come to the jail.

Girls came and went from my pod. They either got released and the whole pod celebrated in the morning as they were called to "roll it up" or they got relocated to a different pod. With the rumor that a certain girl, Lolly, was due in our pod, a 62 was sent around to protest her. The petition worked and she went to pod number five. It seems that Lolly was violent and the others did not want her. I could not believe the power of this form 62. The inmates having a say in matters as this surprised me. I suppose it was better to give the majority small victory than deal with real confrontations later.

I saw Lolly just recently on a city bus. I could not believe that she had on a t-shirt with her name written across the collar in black marker. It made me laugh. If the tattoos on her neck did not give her away as a criminal then this wardrobe choice surely did. We eyed one another warily but said nothing. So the 62 might be ignored completely or it may be a powerful tool. It did not get me any special books that I wanted. The officers probably thought I was a loon. I had asked for history, science, spiritual books, and I even added that I would take any non-fiction that they had. They apparently had nothing; the requesting 62 form was ignored. This lack of quality books is a gigantic problem. The romance novels that lined the shelf were not going to move the girls in the right direction. Out of sheer boredom, if books of importance were available, the girls would at least give them a cursory flip through. That would be better than afternoon shows like *Jerry Springer* and soap operas which only reinforced their bad behavior. I realize the county jail is not a rehabilitation unit, but providing as much positive stimulus as possible seemed like a no-brainer. The county did not care.

I lined up at the door for breakfast as usual one morning and marched the handful of paces into the cafeteria to find that the chairs remained on top of the tables. On this day, we went through the assembly line to get trays, juice, and chicory but snaked right around back into our pod. The rude girls that were in front had saved entire tables in the pod for their friends that lagged behind. This is an example of people not understanding anymore what is rude and what is acceptable. The chairs rightly should be first-come first-served. Somehow the absurd sense of entitlement above others is now the norm. Well, thankfully it is not the norm everywhere; politeness marginally exists in certain places.

I mumbled, "Of course," under my breath and sat on the floor with my back to the wall. As a consolation prize, someone offered me extra milk, I took it. I thought an officer must have called in sick or we were being punished for some reason. After we ate, we stacked the trays near the door. I did not mind. I could crawl back into my bunk sooner. I had taken other's examples and started putting my sheet on the outside of my blanket. The blanket close to my skin kept me warmer. I also folded my blanket in half so as to double it. Anything would help. I was freezing to death. I suddenly wished I was fat.

I only missed a few things besides my favorite foods while I served my days. The main one was my hair dryer. It was horrible on days when I washed my hair. It had to get done about once a week though. The second thing I missed was my feather pillows. I had made them myself and loved them. The flat pillow we were provided only served me to place against the wall to keep from bashing my head against the cement in my sleep. Finally, a computer would have been nice. I thought I needed these things but I did not die without them.

I still wonder why I was placed in the dorm-style building. I heard from the jail veterans that other places in the complex had cells more in keeping with what I had expected. Even more bothersome was the fact that these inmates had access to microwaves. That probably increased the commissary insanity. The people in my pod had to use hot water from the sink to "cook" foods. I found the water in the sinks to be just as satisfactory as the shower water. When I made my hot cocoa or started using single serve coffee packets, the water steamed into the sink. It worked well. Nonetheless, self-righteously I thought if anyone should have been placed in this upper-class holding area, it should have been me. I waited in quiet expectation that I would get moved to this area as the days passed.

It was really a matter of available space not who is more of a criminal than another. I should try to remember that for many people my DUI crime was worse than others, for example, prostitution. As I wrote that last sentence, I was hard pressed to think of anything more accidental than my DUI. The fact that it was the second one makes it seem less accidental no doubt. Here I am being of a denying mind again and self-righteous to boot. It is really all a matter of perspective and of course my own perspective will vote in my favor. Another Scripture verse I tried to keep in mind is, "Whatever situation in which you find yourself, be ye therefore content." (paraphrase- versions mixed) I wish my favorite go-to scripture verses would surface and slap me in the head when I need them the most. I so often only remember them after I act stupidly, rashly, rudely...

The best intentions often (if not most of the time) come to naught. I failed to be content when Lateasha reappeared in the pod. She was back after about a week. There was even talk about her replacing Trish as pod monitor. I liked Trish, for a young girl, she had awesome patience. Lateasha, on the other hand, was the worst pod-mate. Her new bunk was not close to mine but the nighttime shenanigans returned in force with her influence.

A new girl that shared my name moved into the upper bunk near mine. Her feet were at my head. Since we were both tall, this caused middle of the night (or day) over-lap bumps. I wanted to make friends with her since we had something in common. She was half my age though and through observation I decided that she was a beggar and a thief. I was disappointed. I kept trying to see a speck of hope for the girls in the room. Instead I kept falling farther into sadness for them. I could be overly pessimistic because the badly behaved girls obviously drew more attention to themselves making it impossible not to observe them. The girls more like me blended in. I should have spent more time seeking them out for friendship.

The dialogues the girls shared rarely changed. How can we get out of here and back to our way of life faster? Who can we take advantage of to get our way? I even listened in while a group spoke of setting up accidents to sue innocent people for damages. Did this sort of thing really happen? I vowed to watch my back as I went about my business of living after my release. I plan to move to the Pacific Northwest soon. Maybe living at the top of the country will somehow surround me with the top conditions instead of bilge conditions. I often live in fantasy land.

The negativity was contagious among the group. Listening to the constant complaining was exhausting. I heard a girl say that she was so mad because the county was starving her to death. It was difficult to hold my tongue. I enjoyed the food, found it more than adequate, and knew that I was eating better than most people on the planet. Many people that work for a living and pay rent do not even have it so good. I can only imagine the reason God put me in this situation. Shame and guilt gripped me often; self-righteousness had a hold on me. Perhaps I was meant to learn appreciation for the gifts I have received that kept me on the right side of society until now. I was getting a taste of the possibility of how any life can go down a bad road. Only through God's blessings am I able to recognize the cycle. Perhaps I am meant to give something back like the chaplain. I am sure of it but what? How Lord?

Not only the chaplain, but the officers, judges, social workers, and volunteers that submit themselves to this environment for the benefit of society deserve recognition. If they are impatient at times, I no longer begrudge them. There was a male officer in the cafeteria at breakfast time one morning. This first time I was exposed to him, I became angry and I could not shake the feeling all morning. He continuously yelled while we were eating that we had to hurry or go hungry. This was not news to us since five minutes to shovel down the food was all we got. What we did not finish had to get dumped into the trash bin. His droning voice left me wanting to rebel and say to him, "Listen, you may be just one mistake away from being on this side of the situation, so just act human." I suppose I reacted this way because I felt personally affronted as his treating me (as a part of the whole) as an animal. He did not know what each person was in here for. Certainly many of us were horrified at being there and did not fancy the lumping us all together as pieces of trash. Apparently, I was sensitive that morning. I held a grudge against that man all day. This was worse than my feelings toward the curt blonde officer on day one.

Chapter Ten

Marny returned from her turn at recreation as red as a tomato. She was in pain from the burn. She also felt the need to raise her shirt exposing her breasts and dancing around the room that way. This left me disconcerted since she was the beautiful one in the pod and after my "crush" on the bald girl in the cafeteria earlier on, I wished she would stop already. Marny was a stripper before entering jail. Maybe more charges were laid against her because she was in for quite a stay. Girls started talking about how their greatest aspirations for a career were to follow in her footsteps and earn money undressing in clubs. I wonder where the girls I came to know are today.

Besides my run-in with Mercedes at a convenience store, I have spied two other of my pod-mates around the city in the past year. In the awkward position we all find ourselves in of recognizing someone suddenly and showing that in our face, only to wish we hadn't. It was simply a series of glances back and forth but not communication. In both of the cases I hoped the girls did not recognize me in return. I do not regret the experience of being in jail just the ignorant behavior that placed me there. I welcome the memories as an enlightening experience and through these writings hope to prepare other people that fall into the system through an error in judgment. Pre-Madonna types will have a hard time adjusting to the minimalist, military style of life in county jail. Just a note to them, take enough money to place in the docket accounts to buy the luxuries you may want. Do not beg for or steal them.

When a new girl arrived in the section across the aisle in the bed directly opposite Marny, it was not long before a confrontation of fists broke out. Marny was right and I admired her for standing up for herself. She was a tough girl, a likeable one. The new girl was named Valerie. She had been begging for commissary extras from anyone that would listen. When Marny caught her going through her private bin, it was fist to cuffs. The officers came in. taking Marny's word for the event, they removed Valerie immediately. Begging was a serious problem in the pod. I suppose these people behaved the same way out on the street. Who knew?

The worst perpetrator was Gladys. She was the woman I took the greatest disliking to. I even had a confrontation with her one day. She feigned handicap so that she could be called to meals early and if not called ahead of time would barge into the front of the meal line. She weighed about ninety pounds and she was an evil genius.

I spent so much time observing the room that I knew she was no more handicapped than I was. I got sick of seeing her sly smile when she thought she had fooled the others. I was onto her and called her out one morning. She claimed also to be elderly. In reality she was only in her fifties and a quarter of the women were her peers. One day at meal time, the line was formed and she elbowed her way through the line. When she got to where I could talk to her, I plainly accused her of being a fake and a manipulative shrew. I had shocked her by being so bold. She wrinkled up her tiny face and informed me that I was going to Hell. I received appreciative glances from those near me as I rebutted that she was the one headed there between the two of us. She headed back to her bunk probably to munch on her stash of stolen sugar packets. I did not feel particularly remorseful afterward since I thought I had spoken for the entire pod.

Gladys bravely ventured into the bunk section across the aisle from where I laid one day observing the room. If she wanted another argument with me it would have been forthcoming if Marny had not beaten me to the punch. Gladys had a habit of moving her beady little eyes around the room to see what she could take or who she could beg from. This day she blatantly went to an upper bunk, pulled the mattress back and helped herself to a girl's candy. I was moving to sit up and remind her that I was watching her when Marny ran over, grabbed the stolen goods from Gladys' hand and called her a lengthy list of foul names. I wish it had been me to confront her; she was really on my bad side. I simply yelled out, "Good job, Marny." To which I received an evil glare from the retreating thief. Gladys was the only person that I made any vocal judgment against in the pod, otherwise I just observed and my heart sighed. I suppose I was wrong in self-justification.

The girls would line up their out-going letters on the ledge of the bulletin board or viewing partition. When on a field trip to the book shelve or waiting in line at the door, I was amazed at some of the artists in the room. Envelops addressed to family and friends had colored-pencil depictions of animals, forests, self-portraits, and iconography. This craft was healthy and when I saw someone with their pencils out, I talked to them about the art which led them to talk about the mail's recipient. I think they appreciated my interest. I wanted to encourage positive outlets if I could. I was a lot older than most of the girls and sensed they respected me because I generally minded my own business and kept quiet. Most of them realized I was out of place there.

Eva was set to get released. I would miss her. We never shared anything other than pleasant nods of hello to one another, but she was always writing like me and so I liked her. She and I were the only two interested in journaling. At least I did not notice anyone else ever writing. She looked like an angel. Most of the time leaning against her wall; she rarely left her bunk. I know she had children because she would stick pictures that they drew and sent to her on her wall. Their names identified the artists. At shakedown they would get ripped down if she did not have time to pull them herself and hide in a book. I could tell this upset her. Her usually clear face would frown from hairline to chin.

I was proud when Candy approached my bunk to ask on behalf of the girls in their section of bunks if I would move into Eva's vacated bunk. Candy was my age and despite her playful name was quite respectful. I had noticed that their area of the room was generally quiet. I learned that the fact that I was now notoriously quiet was the reason I was invited in. The girls wanted to recruit me before Eva left so as not to get a random noisy, unwelcome mate. At first I was reluctant because I finally had my bunk set up to be free from air-vent wind and it was quite comfortable. The new offer had a vent over the bed. I agreed to move anyway. Carmen, the girl that loaned me the *Left Behind* books would be below me. I did not want to appear ungrateful since I had seen a lot of the girls come and go and the bunk assignments were just chance of whoever asked Trish first. After Candy approached me, I did confirm with Trish. I did not want to be an individual thinker and make her angry. I respected authority and for whatever reason, she was given charge over the forty of us. Linda tried to talk me into staying in her section also because I was quiet. I opted for the change.

I liked the new area. It was in the center as opposed to the other two sections I had lived in which both were closest to the bathroom. My first bunk room was perpetually the loudest because it was farthest away from the viewing windows and the entry door. The girls there thought they could push the limits and they did. They were very inconsiderate. Now, I could see the TV from my bunk if I sat on my heels. I could also immediately know who was entering the pod instead of waiting for the mystery officer's face to appear in the aisle. At times, the officers would enter the pod already yelling but at other times they used stealth to sneak in and find people doing things wrong. Some of these things might be making whip or kissing another girl. The girls in my new area were vocally anti-begging which I liked. If a girl stood in the aisle looking into the bunk area when the girls had their bins out, this meant they wanted a handout. This was their discreet method. Candy and the others would firmly tell them to beat it. I loved it. I am all for giving to people that are in need but they were just fiends. They went to eat in the cafeteria three times a day like the rest of us. I will repeat again the food was good and we were served plenty of it.

Nearing the end of my stay, I was called to the door. In my excitement I arrived without my shoes. The officer scolded me because now she had to wait. Hoping that this summons might have been my release, I was anxious. I should have known better, everyone always left when it was still dark out right after breakfast. In my new bunk in the center area I could not tell what time it was. Before I moved I could see the light or darkness through the rectangular window in the door by the bathroom. Otherwise we lived by fluorescent lights, not the healthiest for the psyche. No one would tell me where I was being taken until the Sally Port driver said he was taking me to medical. I thought it was kind of late now for them to get concerned about correcting my aspirin dose.

Other inmates waited as well. It was a study in hilarity listening to them complain about the wait. They were in jail; their time belonged to the county. Besides where were they going? One was seeing the dentist. We could see the dentist and his assistant preparing for his charges behind glass. The inmates were acting like fools. They yelled at him (the dentist) from this side of the glass to hurry up because they did not have all day. Really? Here is a problem with society today. Why can people no longer wait patiently and entertain themselves internally? It was nearly impossible to hold my tongue during this display. I thought I was at the zoo. Another man raged to me and the air (might as well have just been the air- I willed myself not to hear him) about a tiny bug that crawled about on the floor. He accused the police of keeping him in a sty. All in all this facility was spotless. It was really kind of surprising that I did not spot a single bug of any kind in the mini unit. A miracle really. I wanted to suggest that maybe the bug had fallen off of his own person, but I just observed.

My name was called and I followed a man down the hall and was introduced to a female doctor. She took my weight and asked me questions about my medical history. The weight gain proves how many calories can be burnt through regular plain old living. The job I worked at the time of my arrest and incarceration was a desk job.

It is true what people say about desk jobs, food of all types was continually brought in and placed on the top of the cabinets right in front of my desk, the most convenient place for it. I cursed the practice since it was not convenient for me to smell croissants and donuts without reaching forward and chowing down just to settle back into my comfy chair and do nothing physical.

Even then I remained thin, but laying on the bunk all day only rising for meals was a death wish to my figure. If these are my only problems, I am in pretty decent shape. The reason I had to come to see her was really a required tuberculosis test that the state mandated for every inmate. I thought it funny that they cared about my result just two days before my release. I realized that they did not care but were just satisfying the mandate.

Getting to leave the mini unit even for an hour was nice. The sun was bright and I let my eyes roam over common scenes hungrily. Watching cars on the street, squirrels climbing trees, and watching men mow the grass filled me with desire to get free from my crowded-dark-negative pod. Instead of a movie about aliens growing in giant leaves, a movie should be made about forty girls in a room called pod people.

Chapter Eleven

I was learning about AA and knew that soon I would have to start preparing a fourth step. For those that are unfamiliar with the twelve steps of AA, they are a series of actions to get resentments under control and submit to a higher power in order to permanently give up the alcohol (evil juice). The homework from my sponsor was to memorize the third step prayer while in jail. I did that. It was easy and I love to pray. I moved ahead and wrote out a fourth step on my pad. Later when looking over my notes, I realized that this fourth step was more thorough than the one I did when I got home. The official one took me many tries since my sponsor kept telling me I was doing it wrong. Comparing that one to the jail-time one is interesting. In jail I obviously had more free time. It was very neat and orderly, therapeutic for sure. When I found it, I went over the new (old) fourth step with my sponsor.

The final Sunday afternoon while lazing around in my bunk, I thought I was dreaming when I heard the familiar sound of a NASCAR race coming from the TV area. Wide-eyed, I glanced from one girl to the next willing them not to change the channel. They did not. It was the first time since I had arrived in the pod that my beloved racing was tuned. Football would have been welcome too but this was a real gift. I sat on my knees to see over the top of my wall and watched my boys drive left and fast. To me this was heaven. Jimmie Johnson (Superman) led the field. I looked at the girls sitting around the tables looking up at the screen with new respect. If they liked my favorite sport, they might be alright after all.

I should have known this would end. As soon as my heart rate relaxed from this sudden pleasure, an officer opened the door and told me to roll it up. I was being moved to a different pod. This was in competition for the saddest moment of my jail stay. Like Job of the Bible said , "The Lord gives and the Lord takes away."

I had been in the middle of an interesting Christian book called *Evidence for Jesus.* I placed it on Carmen's bed since she had loaned it to me. She would learn when she returned to her bunk that I was absent. Someone else may even have claimed my bunk by then. I want to search out that book and finish reading it. I would miss Carmen. She was a Christian and involved in AA. So far I have not seen her again.

At this point I was scheduled to leave in two days. I felt a little betrayed. It had taken me so long to get used to my pod-mates only to get thrust into an entirely new group. I am sure no one tried to 62 me out of number six. The authorities had their own reasons. I had to leave quickly and did not say goodbye to the girls I had befriended. The most I could do was wave to them in the cafeteria across the room during meals for the remaining time. Since the officers had confiscated my flat pillow during the last shakedown, it was difficult to carry my mattress, bedding, books, toiletries, and shoes but I proved a contortionist under the disapproving glare of my escort. I would have stuffed it all into the pillow case. I wonder if it was taken on purpose so that I would have to struggle.

I only moved next door. I entered uneventfully. It was unlike my entry into pod six when I had a welcoming committee. If this new pod had a monitor, I did not know who it was. The atmosphere was much different in number five. Number five was quieter. I was lucky and I chose an empty upper bunk in the center area. The pod was different but I was welcomed nicely. After tying my sheets onto my mattress and quickly settling in, I dared to change the TV channel. No one had been in the TV area when I turned the race on but a crabby woman appeared like a ghost when I did. "I'm watching a movie," she said. "I did not know anyone was watching it, sorry," was my gutless reply. I went to my bunk and sulked.

Lolly lived in five. I thought she was nice. Of course, I only observed her for a day. I would be leaving after breakfast the next morning so it barely counted as a day to me. I cheered that it counted as a day to the officials. The lights in this pod were not as bright or else some were burnt out. To my horror, late in the day a girl joined the pod that was even more attractive than the red-head in the cafeteria in the beginning. She also had a shaved head. It was obvious that her hair was dark though and she had blue eyes. It was worse than before. Meals only lasted a few minutes, I had to stay and watch this person laugh, exercise, and interact. I swear I was afraid she or someone would catch me staring at her and punch me out. She was also a gorgeous boy.

I may have been learning the answer to my own question. I was never attracted to girls before. In my own defense both of the two in the pods had shaved heads and looked like males. Still not sure, I temporarily concluded that being in jail may give a person strange ideas about their own gender. It bothered me. I was past ready to see my boyfriends. The sooner, the better. I willed myself to dream about them that night. Three-thirty came and the lights went up. This would be my last meal in the mini unit. Glad to be getting released in a few hours, I was not glad that I would have to buy groceries later that day. I had loved the idea of eating for free. While I worked full-time, I supported myself and food was a problem in my budget. I doubt I would eat so well again for a while. Three meals a day would not be happening on the outside.

I tried to act relaxed while I waited for my release call. With every passing minute I thought I would be staying. I had only been here eighteen days and they had not been too bad but when the appointed day to leave came, I was just as excited as the other girls on their exit days. I secretly feared that I would be overlooked. I did not want to miss the call but also to avoid the nervous anticipation, I tried to get back to sleep. What if they called my name in my former pod? Before I actually left pod six, I said to a few of the girls in there, "If they call my name for my stuff, please remind them of my move." I was not giving the officers any credit to keep track of their charges. Even the best run places make mistakes now and again and I did not want to be one of their mistakes.

Finally they said, "Gilson, roll it up," over the intercom. The girls around me were excited for me and we said goodbye quickly. I dragged my mattress and struggled again with the rest of my things. Everything I was assigned had to get accounted for. I placed my flops, razor, toothpaste, toothbrush, and cup on the ledge where I was told. I had my papers and books with me. I told the officers that the Bible had been a gift from the chaplain and hoped to keep it. They let me but I returned the big blue book. I had one at home. I had many Bibles at home also, but when it came to God's book, the more the merrier.

Anxious to get moving, the torture continued as I watched three officers chow down on donuts and tease each other. I sat on the bench invisible as ever. I wanted a donut. A Sally Port pulled up and a short brown-haired male officer signed some paperwork and I put mini two behind me forever. I loved the sight of the black sky and the stars scattered in the heavens while in New Mexico, but that did not compare to my pleasure at seeing the scene now. I looked up to thank God as much as to look at something besides a cottage cheese textured white ceiling two feet above my eyes. I often look up when thinking about God or praying and the vast sky was a better cathedral.

I watched male inmates doing their laundry jobs while I waited on a bench for my property. I gave up my badge, my orange clothes, and my white sneakers for my brown cords, shoes, and jacket. Seriously, I had been dressed like a candy bar when I was arrested. At last I claimed my purse and contents. Just to check, I looked for my driver's license. Nope. I did manage to leave with a few dollars left in my account. This fact left me out of luck when I asked for a bus pass home. I had seen the person before me secure one just for the asking. The female officer told me that since they knew I have the fare, I had to pay it. Fair enough (pun intended).

I knew right where the bus stop was now. I had enough experience with this court complex to last a lifetime. The first time I left from an overnight here was at my first DUI arrest. It was dark than also and I did not know where I was going. I went the wrong way to get corrected by an officer in a guard shack. Good grief, I did not want any more trouble. I suppose they have so much recidivism they assume everyone knows the drill.

Anxious to move forward in my process, I asked the officer about the probation clerk that I had to meet with within twenty-four hours of my release. She helpfully told me where to find the office but that the clerk was not available until 8:00am. Twenty-four hours was a short time for me because I did not live right around the corner but in the other side of the city. I went to the bus stop in the dark after deciding against waiting for eight o'clock to roll around. I planned to take the bus home and then turn right around and take the bus directly back after looking at my apartment for a minute. I would have plenty of time to look at people living and reacquaint myself with the outside through the bus window on the round trip. This may sound like a waste of time but I would have to return at some point in twenty-four hours anyway. Procrastination might have me napping through the deadline. I hoped there would be a location close to my home that I could attend my monthly check-ins, but when I met with the woman my best choice was the same place as before. Others I had known checked in at a location in the downtown area near where I lived. This did not prove an option for me; I wondered why not but did not ask.

I would have to take two buses to get to the Salvation Army probation location but at least I was familiar. I see my familiarity with the criminal county system as a blessing and a curse. A curse because I have to admit that I can deny it all day but I do have a permanent criminal record now. A blessing because it was an adventure. I also can help those that need guidance when it comes to their questions and expectations.

On the bus ride after finishing processing with the probation woman, I realized that my folder of paperwork was missing. This was like an emergency. All of my legal papers were in that folder. I tugged at the bus's stop cord and got out. Rejecting wasting the time to navigate traffic to the other side of the street to wait for (who knows how long) and catch the bus back, I started walking. As I neared the bus stop, a few other people lazily waited for the next bus. God had kept the wind from blowing my folder contents scattered, kept the curious away, and I walked faster once I saw it there on the edge of the bench. In my mind I said to the people standing around, "Don't touch it, don't touch it. I'm right here." I could have been over-reacting but I was familiar now with the types of people that likely frequent that particular bus stop and these papers were some of the most important papers I have ever been in charge of. I breathed deeply at the bench and said, "Thank God," while holding the folder to my chest like a teddy bear at bed time. I waited with the others as they regarded me as a lunatic. I would rather have gone through my entire life without any brush with the law, but now that it is over, I see the adventure of it.

Afterword

The events recalled in the criminal history story outlined here are written from notes taken while these events were happening, from essays I had written while journaling and memory files. If any aspect of these recording are technically incorrect, they are from the author's ignorance but written with the best effort to remember.

Since enough time had passed since my eighteen day stay in the county jail, I have a new perspective on my statement, "I'm just starting." It was the experience of getting arrested and the road God chose to bring me back to himself that means that I truly am just starting to live the life I had interrupted for a span of time while I pursued my own agenda instead of following His for me. So while my life here is half over, it is really only beginning.

I name this story an adventure and that is a true designation. What is an adventure if not a cultural immersion where a person spends time away from home, their normal routine and encounters forced adaptability. This experience fit that outline and left me a different person. If I was really honest with myself, I can admit that by knowing God I have adventures every day. I do not know what will happen to me around the corner. The best laid plans by man get giggled at by God. There is another Bible verse that says to the effect of, "Man's heart devises his plans but God directs his steps." Now that I am back on track paying attention to Him that created and loves me, I know that the big picture adventure is in its infancy. I'm just starting.

I'm Just Starting 126

Appendixes A-E

Appendix A: Profiles-the pods main personalities

Trish: She served as pod monitor or representative. She often became exasperated with her role. I thought it was too much responsibility for one person given the diversity of girls in the room. I wondered but never found out what the benefit to this job was to her criminal case. She had more patience with complaining, demanding girls than I would have had. She had another job which called her away from the pod daily. She also attended many meetings including Narcotics Anonymous (NA), anger management, and church service. No doubt leaving the pod as often as she could helped to save her sanity from the constant demand.

Tall and lanky, she remained in the same bunk throughout my stay while so many others including me rotated around her. She had more trust in the others than I did. She often left her things laying in plain view on top of her bunk. I hid everything I had under my mattress. A particular habit she had that I find strangely and disturbingly memorable is the fact that she cleaned the inside of her nose with a Q-tip. Similar to the way most people clean their ears. She would dig up into her nostril with the tiny cotton stick. This was a new one to me. I had never seen anyone do that before.

I was surprised to learn that Trish had a girlfriend in another pod in mini two. I was even more surprised when I saw the girl. Trish was the female in the relationship. I never learned the other girl's name but I thought she was nice. A little loud at times but nice. She shared space with me in pod five after my transfer. I could not keep track of who was with whom. It seemed that Trish's girlfriend had another girlfriend as well. I am sure this type of arrangement was common and the basis for a great deal of the fighting I witnessed.

Trish did her job well for a girl in her early twenties. She welcomed me immediately upon my arrival, dealt with the girl's needs adequately, and raised her voice only after the time I would have lost my patience had long passed.

Marny: The most attractive girl in the pod. Marny was about twenty-six years old, was married to a much younger man, and had children outside. I gathered they were from a former marriage. I never learned much about her children. She spoke mostly about her husband whom she had pictures of wedged up into the bottom of the bunk above her. He was very good-looking. He obviously meant more to her at this point in her life than did her kids. In jail for drugs and prostitution, she had a fierce temper. She spent hours lying on her back listening to music. Often she did a type of stretching and calisthenics to the music. The girls danced a lot after lights out, but Marny is the only girl besides pacing Julia that I ever noticed trying to exercise.

She had a shrill tiny laugh and often skipped breakfast. It was funny watching her react when she found a pimple on her face. I suppose she knew she was beautiful although she was super sweet, unless crossed. She was tough and if she was not fighting for herself, she fought for causes and on others behalf. She always ordered much from commissary which she was happy to share. She did not take kindly, however, to people helping themselves to her things. She was my favorite. She still had several more months to serve at the time of my release.

Mercedes: A large girl in her early twenties. She befriended me quickly. She saw my innocence and tried to make me feel comfortable. She taught me what to expect during my stay. She had medium length hair that she changed all the time. She mostly wore curly pig tails and took the effort to primp herself up each day. Guilty of prostitution, Mercedes had an equally voluptuous girlfriend. She shared pictures of her with me. Those made me feel uncomfortable but not too much. Her bin was stuffed with books, sexy underclothes (no idea where she got them from) and luxury hygiene products. She bragged often that she was used to getting anything she wanted from men and that is why she thought she should have the best stuff. She certainly was not going to use county issue toothpaste or shampoo.

She often slept in and skipped breakfast too. I suppose the girls that bought a lot from commissary did not put as much importance on mealtime. It was easy to understand when the call came at 3:30am and with all the noise, it was too soon after anyone got to sleep anyway.

Mercedes had a surprising mothering quality. She also had a manipulative little smile. I could imagine her using it on men. She was peaceful in the pod though and another of my favorites. It was her that inspired the title of this book.

Linda: She was one of the quietest women in my pod until I moved into her bunk area. She was an observer too and concluded that she liked me and turned to confiding in me. It was she that told me I seemed like a reporter. I told her I hoped her words were prophetic. Linda was bitter and withdrawn. Her back always hurt her and she harbored resentments toward her daughter and her husband. She was jailed for dangerous drug charges. She talked often about the happy day when she would get out and could get some of her drug of choice into her system. She was usually calm and talked to herself as opposed to conversing with others. I could relate to that. She was outspoken when riled up though. She rarely made a complaint of her own but piped up loudly in commiseration. I felt badly for her most of anyone when I left. The reason being that she was beyond middle age and although she may have the chance and the drive to come clean, I felt her time was running out. The stories she had about her family seemed delusional. If they were half-true it is understandable why she would want to alter her mind state. Linda rarely ate anything. She did not beg or steal and I liked her.

Marty: I had trouble putting my finger on Marty. She was in her fifties I would say and quite mean. It was a front though because she warmed up to me once my stay was half over. She and I never made friends but she ceased glaring at me with the evil eye. My feet in her face the first few days really put me on her bad side for a while. She had a girlfriend and they would have tiffs that were entertaining for me if not frustrating for her. She handled her fights with her girlfriend (who was in the pod also) like a petite flower. This went against her outward appearance of toughness. She was a master hair-braider and always had a client on her bunk. She fought quite often but only with words. I have no idea what her crime was.

    Cora: This girl was about twenty-five years old. She arrived when I already lived in the pod for a week. The relationship between her and Marty developed after this. At first I noticed no interaction and then typical couple behavior. I knew they were an item when I saw them cuddling and kissing by the rectangular door window. They often tried to stay together in Marty's lower bunk but Cora always made a jump for her upper bunk near me if the threat of an officer entering came. I liked Cora very much. Her voice was deep like a man but other than that she appeared more feminine than Marty. She acted introverted and her identity in the pod was completely based on her affair with Marty. Her long hair was in dreads which she let hang loose or put in a tail gathering. I liked it. I wondered what she thought about the constant hair-braiding transfers between the other girls. They sometimes made trains of girls on the floor one behind the other combing and braiding. It must be a pain in the rear end to have the texture of hair that requires so much maintenance.

    Cora rarely talked and then only to defend herself against Marty's accusations. She was meticulously clean and groomed although she did not bother with the absurd primping like many some of the others. She had a strange habit of putting her socks on and taking them off over and over again. It kind of endeared me to her. I have no idea whether she liked me, was indifferent toward me, or hated me.

    Ricky: A girl with hope. Ricky scolded the others for their behavior often but since she was pregnant and turning over a new leaf, she did not fight. She read a lot which I admired in the noisy room. She enjoyed the romance novels that I rejected repeatedly but any reading is better than none. She played with her hair a lot but was understated and conservative. It is hard to name someone as conservative in fashion and grooming when we all had the same or similar clothes on and mostly the same toiletries. I just got that impression of her. That she may be a tom boy on the outside and that she did not bother with fancy styles or make-up. It is quite funny how a person (myself) makes judgments about the girls/women without knowing them in real life at all. It is a skewed circumstance. I fancied myself a bit of a philosopher while I was there because I wrongly judged myself as smarter than ninety percent of the others. This was a terrible injustice to them and a great sin on my part. I did not know them at all or anything about them. Shame on me, but I still did it continuously.

Ricky was thrilled about her coming baby. She wanted to go straight for his/her sake. She did not know the gender but had hoped for a boy. She had little patience for the noise and stupid behavior of the others. She kept her head buried under her covers a lot which had me laughing often about how she was breathing under there. I let the small things entertain me.

Lateasha: Probably my least favorite girl in the pod. She was loud, rude, arrogant, and crabby. These traits were all present but physically she was a beautiful black girl. She was expelled from the pod via a 62 form at which I was happy but when she returned she suddenly was nominated as Trish's replacement as monitor. Thank goodness that did not happen. Anarchy would have been the name of the game even worse than it already was. She fancied herself a future stripper and frequently gave the pod a preview of her technique whether we wanted it or not. She sang loudly all night long with her headphones on. The headphones should not have been available for two reasons. The girls were spoiled by the luxury and it heightened their rudeness. No one was getting any sleep in that pod at night. Lateasha saw herself as a princess and with a cleaner attitude she may have been a quality person. She liked to fight and anything would set her off.

JoAnn: This girl seemed like one of the most hopeless of the lot. Very young and obstinate, she could not wait to get out to commit more crimes. She was involved in drugs and battery. From listening to her talk it seemed she had her hand in a crime ring that involved not only her boyfriend but also her mother and brothers. Returning to that environment after her release would surely have her returning to jail real soon. She got released early on in my stay. She was one of the first that I witnessed of the buildup and release morning anticipation. She constantly washed her hair. It made me colder just looking at her. I guess this was her entertainment, washing and combing her hair. Her lower bunk was like a club at all hours of the day and night. Up to six girls would cozy up onto the bunk and hang out. Listening to them create new crimes to pursue after they left was depressing. JoAnn was so young, I hope she was only bragging to impress the others and her heart really was a little less vicious than she let on. It is sad that they used so much bad to impress instead of striving to be better people.

These girls were true victims of their environments. They were surrounded by crime and dysfunction and did not know what normal behavior was. Sadly, I think society as a whole is taking this road with the universal ignorance of God's word and popular non-acknowledgment of him.

JoAnn's boyfriend had robbed and beaten a man while I was in the pod and he was brought into the jail. JoAnn and the others that clutched with her swore revenge upon the system that brought him back (again) into jail. Talk about misplaced anger. This was an insane culture.

Gladys: I was wrong about Lateasha as my least favorite, I forgot for a minute about Gladys. The skinny old woman was a fraud, a thief, a beggar, and a manipulative soul in a ninety pound body. She had an affinity for eating sugar packets. I never saw her indulge in the whip creations though, strange. That was probably because no one wanted to share with her because she constantly stalked the room hovering to find things to steal. She faked a handicap to get into the cafeteria first and sit at a head table. She was as spry as any one of the rest when she though no one was looking. I was always looking. I never saw her do anything other than case each person's area. She did not read, watch TV, play games, or write. She was like a tiny minion. One day when I could not keep my mouth closed any longer, I told her my opinion of her.

Marny 2: The older Marny seemed normal and pleasant until I realized that she was the passive aggressive type of person that smooched up to each person differently to set herself in the best light. Her personality was not at all consistent. She was about forty-five years old with jet black hair. She changed her long style several times each day but was not involved in the braiding trend. She tried to keep up with the younger women by dancing throughout the night. She was a whip maniac and also the leader of the tarot card phenomenon. I know she was a thief because she stole a pair of socks that I had kept hidden. She brazenly started wearing them as if she had not stolen them. I let it go, I did not want to become what I hate which is a fighter. Maybe I was afraid the brute would beat me up. She was super friendly one minute and glaring at you with hatred the next. I do not think anyone was unhappy when she got released. It prompted a broad change in bunk dynamics. This led me into the second bunk room I lived in across the aisle from the first.

Candy: A simple woman about my age, I liked Candy. Her hair was worn long and in a ponytail. She was refreshingly straight and had a husband waiting for her outside. Like most of the older girls she was well adjusted to her current fate. She did fight verbally often. She was outspoken about the immaturity, irresponsibility, and rudeness of the younger girls. It was she that had started the 62 petition to have Lateasha removed from the pod. She was strict with her commissary supplies but shared with her favorites. She scolded Gladys quite often and told her repeatedly to get out of her (Candy's) area. She knew that Gladys was simply stalking and begging so she reminded her (Gladys) that she had no business in that area and to get out. Candy personally came to my bunk to request my move into her bunk area. She and the others had voted on me. This made me feel loved.

Carmen: My age only prettier, blonde Carmen was the nearest to my own background, current troubles, and spiritual convictions. She had tons of good books and she allowed me to help myself to her bin to browse them whenever I wanted. She also recently started attending AA and I enjoyed sharing conversations with her about God.

Eva: She arrived when I had been in the pod about a week. Unlike the really young girls, Eva had her headphones on most of the time but listened to them privately without the loud singing that some of the others insisted on subjecting the pod to. She had a wide face like a cat and wore her long hair in a ponytail. The hair ties must have been sold at the commissary because I couldn't imagine where they came from at first.

Eva wrote letters to her children often and received some in return. She often decorated her wall with pictures they drew only to have them ripped down by the officers. I fail to find any reason for this at all. Eva always became listless after this happened. She stayed up most of the night and read in the dark. I do not know how she did this. She must have had see-in-the-dark cat's eyes to match her wide cat face. She sketched pictures that I was really impressed with. It was a positive outlet. She did not seem like much of a criminal. I think she was in for a drug charge.

Sue: A jolly fun woman of about twenty-five, Sue was so likeable the judge probably had trouble convicting her. If she wasn't laughing she was singing (nicely) or smiling and telling jokes. She had a job and returned to the pod very late with goodies. The goodies were either snacks or messages from friends to my pod-mates. She wanted to get out as fast as possible to be with her children. She spoke of them often and just glowed when she did.

Mary: Built strong and solid like a man, Mary always smiled and was popular with everyone in the pod. She liked to act like the boyfriend of the others in my area. They always joked about it and kissed each other lightly. She was so bouncy and happy, I did not mind. Her hair was like a red brush cut. When haircut time came around, she got a fresh close trim. I wanted so badly to rub her head like I did to all the men I knew that wore that style. I did not want there to be any mistake about my preferences however. The last thing I would have wanted or needed would have been for one of these girls to gain a crush on me. Mary left the pod only about a week after my arrival.

Lynn: This was JoAnn's shadow. Lynn agreed with all of the crazy things JoAnn said and mimicked her hair styles daily. She was very young and wanted badly to fit in. She was one of the prettiest girls and I think she planned to use that fact to get through life.

Brett: This girl was like a tornado through the pod. She was one of the girls that had to remain in a bunk by the clear partition for the guards to watch closer than the others. The tattoos on her neck were some of the most blatant and she looked like a scary character despite her tiny stature. She seemed to appear in the pod after about a week and everyone knew her. She never bothered me personally but she gave me the impression that she really needed to be in one of the front bunks. Many of the girls seemed to be her girlfriend. She really enjoyed the notoriety of being on the guards watch list. I believe there was little hope for her on the outside.

Appendix B: Profiles- The Officer Guards

Crasin: This petite blonde woman had a superiority complex. It extended not only above the inmates but to the other officers as well. She thought that by wearing a bow in her hair and a lot of makeup that her huge hind-end would be diminished. She did not have a smile for anyone, not even her fellows. She was mean and snotty. She mostly remained in the desk area dealing with administration but she would occasionally take us to the cafeteria for meals or commissary pick-up. I feel badly for her husband if she has one.

Arnold: This woman came on like a freight train but I learned that she was sweet inside. She had a catcher's mitt face and a formidable figure. She was a great officer. She knew when to be serious and when to slack off a bit. She was respected because of this. It was she that gave me the wrong pill and stressed me out but she personally did not flub up the medicine, she just delivered it.

Smith: Smith was a lot of punch in a tiny package. Her short brown hair sat atop her tiny head which got lost in the whole because for a short woman her legs were very long. The petite woman had a loud voice and used it often to scold and give orders. She entered the pod and walked around often which I liked. I felt that she cared about her job responsibilities while not taking herself too seriously. Most of the other officers would yell from the door and guessed at happenings inside the pod, too disinterested to walk through.

I often observed Smith with a betraying smile on her lips when she tried to be firm and enforce some rule she agreed was silly. She knew what really mattered and did not sweat the small stuff while letting us know with her tone when she meant business.

Billings: This black woman stood way above any of the girls in the pod and the other officers. She was sweet and always had her make-up perfectly applied. She looked fresh no matter what time of day I saw her. She was likeable. It was her that was in charge both times I went outside. She must have liked getting out personally also because the others offered any excuse to keep us in. She made small talk with the women in the pod and only raised her voice when she really lost her patience.

Levine: Another likeable officer, she yelled a lot but with a certain air of respect that we were human beings. She was approachable and would do what she could to get answers for us and treated us well. She was an excellent officer. She respected her responsibility and other people. She must have been exemplifying Jesus as no respecter of persons.

Appendix C: Jail notes-verbatim

Finally paper- 4th day

Day before

Bus in- spilt snax

Girls Food-times

Guards

Pod

Clothes change

Cold

Commissary

Shower/ loo/ sink

Classes- AA- delay   Substance abuse, self-defeating,anger management, church

Rec time

Whip

Girl below-not like me at first

██████ (████,████?) leaving 4am on Sunday

Flip-flop ear plugs

Strip search- took my nylon knee highs

Lock down

Women all ages- no make-up, hair dryers, ect.

Hair braiding

Pregnant girls- xtra mattress, milk, extra food

window- door with small opening

surprise super clean floresant (sp) lite cover

████, ████, ████ (pretty), ████, ████, ████, ████, ████, ████, █ ████, ████, ████, ████ (assistant rep), ████, (new), ████, ████, ████, ████, ████, █ ████

Sally Port

Lites on/off

Books-not really

Medical situation

Types crimes- prostitution, battery, attempted murder, trafficking, bad checks, counterfeiting, shoplifting, violation probation/parole, DUI

TV, cards, games, radios

Leaving days-yeah-court times for girls

Underwear- multiple pairs

Coffee-hot water- soup- whip

Footwear- reg, flip-flops, no toe flip-flops, white sneakers, orange shoes, inmates own shoes

Every (not the side ones in bunk area but) doorway (interior/exterior) and windows- archways identified with numbers, very military

███ lost orange shirt during shake down- got upset- bigger issues came out about the incarceration

Loudspeaker

Coffee-chicory

Tie sheets

Pod ceiling- cottage cheese- pure white

Need to stretch

Various types shoes littered everywhere

Games- sorry, monopoly, backgammon, scrabble, uno, cards,

Church-Catholic, Pentecostal, Jehovah Witness, Bible Study, Mother boon (?)

-whisker growing- no tweezers- finally pulled out with nails-something to do

Tarot cards

Laundry

Some are real slobs- no flush, leave blood on toilet, wrap shower nozzle with maxi pad??

-air conditioner broken-praise the Lord –some of these girls complaining so much about being frozen now are complaining of the heat. Gimme a break

Work- kitchen, sewing, cleaning offices

Pod cleaning- each day after lunch- take turns- girls do it without complaining

Tempted to doodle on wall by my bunk- but not good idea

Springer- General Hospital

Young girls- issues- funny- they're clueless- but nice

Urinals in bathroom- used to be man quarters

One girl vigilante was running outside and pacing inside

Keep picking up same novels and rejecting them- I wonder how long it will keep up if I don't get the books I want

Funny what some of the things the girls spend $ on at commissary that they see as necessary essentials

This entire DUI experience is leading to positive ends

AA friends- needed sobriety- return to faith

Serenity prayer- helped me break from TW

Jail- observation builds wisdom and time on my hands allows me to re-familiarize myself with scripture

Proverbs 6:27- "You can't shovel fire into your lap without getting burned." (NIV)

Trading food in mess hall- only about 5 minutes to eat

I think I'm the only girl in here without tattoos- whoops- no couple others

Tues- drama about the air being broken- then fixed –plumbing- girls complaining their criminal asses off

The girls are sending around a 62 petition about conditions in mini 2

They do not understand jail/ inmate dynamics. There are too many criminals and there is no other housing.

Furthermore- many people that pay good rent live in worse places. They are being a little dramatic to say the least

New girl came in (Tues) talking about her experience in ███ 15 years ago- God don't let that be me

Everybody is gaining weight- commissary-42 pieces bread week (rice, potatoes)

███ loaned me *Pilgrim's Progress.* I like it, always wanted to read it, ███ only had romance novels, I had to decline her offer.

I got replies about the classes I wanted to attend, plus my own big book- I have already read ███ but the more the merrier.

Tues nite 19th- even took socks off, finally nice and warm

Gave me aspirin this morning even though I didn't sign the sheet- it is getting late and they have not called for second med call

Girl in loo told me that I look so innocent; I said I feel so innocent but inside I said I'm guilty

Waking up on the 6th day is weird- one of the officers must have called in- had to bring breakfast (SOS) trays back to room. I ate sitting on floor because ███ had saved herself and girlfriends seats at the table without (before) even going into mess hall- I did score two extra milks- yummy

The air is still out, it feels great- My hair is filthy- better wash it today causa the air being off it won't be so bad.

Day 6- getting my groove on now- pretty much got the hang of everything- no rec again today- that's no fresh air 4 days

*The air is broken- I reckon God is answering my prayer

Envelop	.60
Coffee	.90
Hot Cocoa	1.05 (2)
Candy bars	1.98
Pencil	.20
	4.73

Besides the obvious freedom, privacy, and good food(sic), things I missed the most in county jail

Computer, hair dryer, and my pillows

Real coffee-tap water, chicory

Computer to write

What is the hope in the future for the young girls in here?

1.   Their affinity for ink/ tattoos will keep many career opportunities closed

2.   I haven't heard remorse for their crimes in their stories, just how to manipulate system to ease their punishment and that they will return to the same way of life afterward

3.   I will pray individually for them; I wonder about their family dynamics

4.   They are talking about causing accidents to sue innocents for$$- I hope they would never do something like that

6th day dinner- Shocked and distracted- in mess hall- (a girl-shaved head), very young- looked like a gorgeous boy- shame on me- I couldn't keep my eyes off of her. I think I could have trouble sentencing someone so young and pretty- she was a gorgeous boy.

American Idol- frenzy

Officer said ▮▮▮ had to remove picture reminding her of her kids off the wall

▮▮▮▮- a girl that was to be transferred in with us got boycotted. The officers were sympathetic and let the girls petition for NOT having her house with us

-typical day

-Guards smoking outside window- smell driving some crazy

Thur. May 21st- Good lunch today- turkey, coleslaw, pasta salad

-been in lock down most of the day- lots of arguing among the girls

-self-defeating behavior class was awesome

Chapters

Acknowledgments- Introduction   or just 1-10

Surrender

The girls

The guards

The routine

Hope for future?

Entertainment

What we think we need, but really don't

Reader's Digest

Editor-in-chief- █████████

Feature Editors- █████████, █████████, ████

█████

Senior Editor- █████████

-does not accept unsolicited article length manuscripts BUT:

Readersdigest.com/funnyjokes- jokes, headlines, lists, ect- if published in print edition- $100 paid

Gladwells Five Steps to Success:

1. Find meaning and inspiration in your work
2. Work hard
3. Discover the relationship between reward and effort
4. Seek out complex work to avoid boredom and repetition
5. Be autonomous and control as much of your own destiny as possible

Today is Friday, one week ago at this time I was being processed into this place.

It is May 22, my 3 month sobriety date. This morning, I received the wrong med. I said to them- This doesn't look right- █████ (?) blonde stocky guard said "it's right," but with my medical history- I'm a bit nervous. Should I make a 62 (?). Don't want to cause trouble- but neither do I want to pay for some expensive drug or have a mystery drug in my system

-I filled out the 62- stating my concern- then retracted it- If wrong, I will refuse it tomorrow.

Plus I found a good science book that just arrived on the shelf- I'm sticking it under my mattress; not that anyone in here is interested in that type of thing.

-Following ████████ lead, I moved to the "home" across the aisle where it is quieter. The others hopefully aren't resentful, but they are bloody loud at night. They are all real young and don't realize their noise level and that the older girls and the pregnant girls need sleep. When breakfast was called this morning- I felt drunk I was so tired after only getting about one hour of sleep. It seems some others in the dorm are petitioning to get the loud ones removed. It is not a single person that you can pinpoint, just the combined camaraderie. Not to mention, we have not been allowed rec, fresh air, and daylight for a week- creates restlessness

-another story for my drunken progression list

www.aagrapevine.org

Ham on Wry- contributions/ submissions

Human editor

P. O .Box 1980

475 Riverside Dr. New York, NY 10115 or

gveditorial@aagrapevine.org

Joke: A slice of pizza is in the stomach waiting to be digested. Suddenly a shot of whiskey barrels down. The pizza lets it pass in front of him. A few minutes later, another shot of whiskey comes through. Courteously, the pizza lets it pass in front of him too. A few minutes later a third shot of whiskey tumbles into the stomach. The pizza says to the whiskey, "What's going on up there?" "They're having a great party," says the whiskey. "Really?" responds the pizza, "I think I'll go up there and take a look."-Jay C.

Joke: A husband and a wife were sitting in their living room. He said, "Just so you know, I never want to live in a vegetable state, dependent on some machine and fluids from a bottle, if that ever happens, just pull the plug". His wife got up, unplugged the TV and threw away all of his beer. - Tim

██ mentioned that I remind her of an undercover journalist in here. Apropos- encouraging.

I'm just starting- my response to ██████

-put some paper into the air conditioner grate in ceiling today- I hope the guard doesn't notice but so cold, I couldn't help it.

I like it since I moved to this side of the room. Last night- May 22, it was as quiet as can be in here. I have AA finally tonight.

I just missed laundry call again – I was fixing to get my stuff into the bag a few minutes prior- the police came and snatched it. Now I'll have to wait until Tuesday. I don't stink yet though; at least I don't think so.

-Wow, I got a jail haircut today. Saved twenty bucks but the bangs are still a little long, my fault; she asked me if I wanted them shorter.

AA class today also- it was nice.

New girl on next bed- ██████- real nice

Today is Sunday (24th?). Officer said we are going to have rec today.

Even though I got that whisker out earlier this week,, I feel more (like 3) and they are vexing me- can't get them out yet.

Order 5/24	
Candy bars	1.98
Coffee	.90
Hot Cocoa	1.05
Envelop	.60

Jail is a good study for a psychiatrist or psychologist- thought of that because of sphere (?) and realized I would be a good one (good insights but no real remedies)

-World in a snap

Grimes books- let her go, stranger reminds me of people on highway that you keep passing smiling and waving and you feel a loss when they get off at a different exit than you.

██████ and I witnessed ████ stealing from?? ████ confronted her. Big controversy- good- I know that woman is manipulative.

Shakedown- removed from room- █████ said put your hair up- I protested and she said, "Just do it." ██████ loaned me a hair tie. I reckon there is a lice scare in this dorm- yikes.

██████ cut her hair and it is like when ████ first gets his done. I want to go rub it, but that seems inappropriate.

Seven more full days- not too bad so far. An interesting and profound experience.

Rec today- only eight from unit- █████ got burnt, she looks like a tomato, maybe my turn will come tomorrow.

5/25- slept almost all day- the rec shouldn't wipe me out that much, just walked, my period must be coming. █████ let me use her thermal since my shirt is in laundry. She's so sweet. It's commissary tomorrow- I am dreaming of that <u>candy</u>!! I had a dream about █████ again last night. That is the 3rd one- ████ and ████ were in a different dream last night and ████ (██████) was in my dream just now.

███████- girl my age and pretty- I like her, she just approached me to talk about AA. Too bad she lives in ████████.

I have been sleeping the day away again but today is our cleaning day.

Two stubborn whiskers, I still can't get out- INSANE- Three Musketeers Tonight.

Laundry's back- my t-shirt is not back, bra and socks only. Someone stole my new t-shirt.

3rd bed change- this one away from AC vent. Hopefully it will be better.

Everyone fighting over rec. ██ wants her own way.

██ is having a problem with bunk assignments- too many obnoxious girls and girls that don't get along in here. Glad I am leaving soon.

Whoops- skipped a page.

Why are there so many lesbians in jail? Are they prone to be criminals? If yes, then why? If not why does (if it does) jail drive the girls to become lesbians??? It is kind of like which comes first, the chicken or the egg.

Had to go to medical this morning for mandatory routine physical-can't believe the complaining girls over there. I got a tuberculosis test.

Girl asked me to move to different bunk area today, since ██ got released and her bunk vacated. I feel so wanted. ██ and █ were sad that I left. Everyone likes me because I am quiet.

Drunken episode- Homestead- fall down stairs drank and drove than climbed a big tree by bonfire.

I only have 5 days left- tomorrow is candy bar night again.

My t-shirt came up in the laundry finally. That means someone must have taken it the other day- Oh well, I have it now.

-finished *Left Behind* and will read *Tribulation Force* next.

-another girl named ██ is now in the next bunk.

-another dream about ██.

R-May 28th

I can't believe that these girls complain about the food. They say, "Like the noodles are over- cooked," Are they kidding me? "They are starving me." Really?

██ (pretty) and ██ had a fight over ██ begging for commissary.

Will Travel with Consequences –

███████ took full advantage of her first day in Cape Town. Exhausted she laid her pack on the carpet, sunk into a cushy chair in the day room of her hostel and said, "Hi," to the man lying on the couch watching television. She had wanted this trip for a couple of years and had finally planned it. Little did she know that the man she had befriended ████ (just one of his names), would turn out to be a fraud. He would eventually cost her a career, a home, a child, her money, her dignity, and her faith in people.

-████, ████ adoptions-tie together. That's the selling point. What about ████?

-bus system

Will Travel with Consequences

Drunken Episodes- how I was sure my life had become unmanageable

I'm Just Starting- a woman's mistake sends her to jail for the first time at 43.

The Cage- staff

Shitski man- It's Sunday- only 2 days left. Been sleeping mostly and then was reading. And then I heard the race on TV. BONUS- I thought . One hundred laps in, I get a call to roll it up because I was being moved to pod 5, to an unfamiliar place for my last day. No more race for me and I have to get used to a whole new bunch of girls- shit.

I didn't even get a chance to say goodbye to all the other girls especially ███████. Oh well, I am not in control of my own destiny in here. It is what it is. I also had to return *The Evidence for Jesus*. The book I had just borrowed from ███████. It was really good too. Oh well, everything happens for a reason, maybe I should try to get a job with NASCAR. How? I don't know.

5/31- This new bed is kind of cold. There was a shakedown and the law took my pillow (?). The pencil sharpener in pod five doesn't work. So, I won't be able to write much. I am now ready to be done here.

June 1st- My last day- out in the morning I hope, I think. I have to get this probation business set up (near home please). I need to find about attending a victim impact panel. I will be very glad to get off of bus 52 in front of my house. I don't have any food at home, I reckon some time tomorrow, I will have to get some groceries.

Three Musketeers and M&Ms tonight- my treats, yummy. I can't wait to step into my Roswell shoes. I wonder if I will take or leave the two large books I got from the programs and the chaplain. I really don't want to carry them around. We'll see.

Smoking in moderation for God's sake- okay!!

Food- Atkins-avoid hunger, need less food

Alcohol- ha-ha, no more drinking, <u>no cost</u>!

Rent	$450
Electric	$40
Phone	$55
Cable	$45
Counseling	$100
Probation	$55
Bus pass	$55
Living	$150
Total	$950 @ 1,000 month

Big Book Acceptance page 417

Acceptance is the answer to all my problems today. When I am disturbed it is because I find some person, place, thing, or situation- some fact of my life- unacceptable to me, and I find no serenity until I accept that person, place, thing, or situation as being exactly the way it is supposed to be at this moment. Nothing, absolutely nothing happened in God's world by mistake.

Most (65%) of Americans do not indulge in alcohol. I certainly can be one of them. Strangely (unbelievable to the saturated [no pun intended] drinker) I will then be in the majority and living normally- the drinkers are the minority.

Appendix D: Gospel of Jesus Christ

Jesus Christ is God's son and was born of a virgin through the power of the Holy Spirit. His mission on earth was to reconcile man's relationship to God. All men are sinners and cannot enter heaven as sinful creatures. Jesus Christ shed his blood (being perfect, holy, and sinless) through his crucifixion to take ALL of man's sin upon himself. Salvation is a free, loving gift of God given through grace alone to anyone that will accept it and turn to Him. Jesus became cursed in our place and was resurrected from the dead on the third day. He is the first of the resurrection and those that believe in Him will follow Him in the resurrection and gain eternal life.

I urge everyone to study the Bible in its entirety to learn about God. "In the beginning was the Word, and the Word was with God and the Word was God"(John 1:1 KJV). "The Word was made flesh and dwelt among us" (John 1:14 KJV). "All scripture is given by inspiration of God, and is profitable for doctrine, for reproof, for correction, for instruction in righteousness" (II Timothy 3:16 KJV). The Old and the New Testament are compatible and should be studied in concert. For those that are brand new to the Bible, good starting points are the gospel according to John and the book of Romans written by Paul. I hope you will learn to love the scriptures and the more you read and study the more you will want to search through the pages.

Appendix E: Twelve Steps of Alcoholics Anonymous

1. We admitted we were powerless over alcohol, that our lives had become unmanageable.

2. Came to believe that a power greater than ourselves could restore us to sanity.

3. Made a decision to turn our will and our lives over to the care of God, as we understand Him.

4. Made a searching and fearless moral inventory of ourselves.

5. Admitted to God, to ourselves and to another human being the exact nature of our wrongs.

6. Were entirely ready to have God remove all these defects of character.

7. Humbly asked Him to remove our shortcomings.

8. Made a list of all persons we had harmed, and became willing to make amends to them all.

9. Made direct amends to such people wherever possible, except when to do so would injure them or others.

10. Continued to take personal inventory, and when we were wrong promptly admitted it.

11. Sought through prayer and meditation to improve our conscious contact with God, as we understand Him, praying only for knowledge of His will for us and the power to carry that out.

12. Having had a spiritual awakening as a result of these steps, we tried to carry this message to alcoholics, and to practice these principles in all our affairs.

Andrea M. Gilson is a new author. She plans to live next in the Pacific Northwest to continue writing and learning while enjoying nature. *I'm Just Starting* is her second book following *Will Travel with Consequences*. She has articles published in The St. Petersburg Times, SW FL Parent & Child Magazine and several on-line sources. Visit her website at www.andreamgilson.com.

I'm Just Starting 158